Arizona Wildlife Views
Special Edition
Arizona Game and Fish Department

D060112B

TABLE OF CONTENTS

GEORGE ANDREJKO

JOHN CANCALOSI

GEORGE ANDREJKO

PREFACE

When the Arizona Heritage Fund was created in 1990, the Arizona Game and Fish Department gained much needed financial support to assist us in reaching critical goals for the state's wildlife. Providing more and better information

about wildlife was one of those goals. With assistance from the new funding source, many planned for but previously unfunded publications could finally become a reality—publications that would help Arizona's citizens to understand and appreciate their extraordinary wildlife heritage. Beginning in 1992, *Arizona Wildlife Views,* the Department's flagship magazine, published a series of special issues dedicated to this purpose. These issues quickly became bestsellers. In fact, orders soon exhausted supplies, much to the dismay of wildlife advocates across the state, who have continued to request that we reprint the issues to satisfy unmet demand. Now, with the support of the Heritage Fund, we present a revised compilation of the most requested special issues—the birds, bats, herps, hummingbirds, and game species of Arizona—the best of *Arizona Wildlife Views.*

A TRIBUTE TO HERITAGE

By Terry B. Johnson, Nongame Branch Chief

GEORGE ANDREJKO

Of the many things that one generation can pass on to the next, perhaps most important is an environment that offers a full range of options from which to choose. The choices made are what make each person's life unique, distinct even from those of parents, siblings, or progeny. Each family can help create many aspects of that environment at home. But, away from home, it takes far more than a village to raise a child. Clean air, clean water, and a landscape rich in forests, grasslands, desertscrub, aquatic systems, and wildlife reflect our stewardship decisions as a

DAN CONWAY

nation, in fact, as a world community. Our steward-ship legacy will be a full range of choices, or not. Thus it goes, each generation upholding, or diminishing, the next one's public trust.

In 1990, Arizonan's spoke loudly and clearly about the need to protect their public trust, as a natural legacy for those who would follow. By an overwhelming major-ity, voters approved the Heritage Initiative to set aside $20 million in Arizona Lottery revenues each year for parks, trails, and natural areas, historic preservation, and a full range of wildlife conservation activities. Al-though a few dissenters have tried to undo what the voters approved, the Arizona Heritage Fund has survived, so far.

Meanwhile, each year the Ari-zona Game and Fish Department and the Arizona State Parks Board have invested their respective $10 million Lottery allocations in projects that carry out the voters' will. As you browse this book, you will see some of the wildlife spe-cies that have benefited from this investment in the future. We hope you enjoy this collection of the spe-cial issues of *Arizona Wildlife Views* magazine, and the underlying reality of the Arizona Heritage Fund, *Lottery Dollars Working for Wildlife*. Your wildlife. Your children's wildlife. Your grandchildren's wildlife.

ARIZONA'S WILDLIFE LEGACY

By Terry B. Johnson, Nongame Branch Chief

Clichés run rampant in the wildlife world, and none seems more common than any given state's claim to having the "most unique" and "unsurpassed abundance" of animal life within its borders. Each state has also arrived at some form of "ecological crossroad," where, in most un–Kipling like fashion, East meets West and North meets South. And so it is with Arizona, which lies where the northern Rockies meet the southern Sierra Madre Occidental, and where the Great Plains and Chihuahuan Desert give way to the Great Basin and Mohave and Sonoran deserts. This Southwestern crossroad sprawls across a rugged landscape that rises from just above sea level near Yuma to more than 12,000 feet atop the San Francisco Peaks. The landscape is broken by rivers, some of which still flow year–round, incised by canyons that defy belief, and cut nearly in half by the remarkable Mogollon Rim. No other state lays claim to four deserts, the world's longest continuous ponderosa pine forest, the Grand Canyon, or the "Rim" made famous by Zane Grey.

Arizona's wildlife heritage is also, of course, appropriately and truly unique, though in truth a few other continental states do have a greater variety. Florida, Texas, and California come to mind. However, quantity is not everything, and we hold that the quality of Arizona's wildlife, much like the quality of human life in Arizona, may indeed be unsurpassed by other states. We think that you will probably feel the same way, after reading this book, in which we capture a fair representation of Arizona's amphibians, reptiles, birds, and mammals.

First, though, a word of warning. Not every animal native to or introduced into Arizona is described herein. We have not even included all the native animals for which the Arizona Game and Fish Department is responsible, let alone all the exotics and the countless insects and other invertebrates residing in our state. Given that Arizona is home to more than a thousand kinds of crustaceans, mollusks, fishes, amphibians, reptiles, birds, and mammals, a book of this size is not up to the task of describing everything.

So, for this effort, we have extracted some of our favorite material from past "special"

GEORGE ANDREJKO

issues of *Arizona Wildlife Views*, the Department's bimonthly magazine. Even though the limits of space have allowed us to present only a portion of our wildlife species, we hope that the variety covered here will inspire you to look deeper on your own and learn more about the species that we could not include this time around. If you do, you will likely become as captivated as we are by the beauty, behavior, resilience, persistence, and the wonder of Arizona's wildlife. Then, when that wildlife needs human help, you will likely be someone they, and we, can count on.

And make no mistake about it: Wildlife does need our help, because Arizona is at a "quality of life" crossroad, as well. Such great numbers of us have made Arizona our home that little of the landscape is not marked by our presence, and more of us arrive every day. How we manage the growth will determine the quality of our natural environment, and affect the abundance of our wildlife legacy to future generations. Wildlife cannot move elsewhere when humans move in; it must adapt, or vanish. When the latter happens sufficiently frequently, species become rare, even "endangered." And humans realize that some of what they moved here to enjoy no longer exists, simply because they moved here to enjoy it.

Our job at the Arizona Game and Fish Department is not to stop human population growth, urbanization, and other impacts on the land and wildlife, but to help manage them. Our mission, "To conserve, enhance, and restore Arizona's diverse wildlife resources and habitats through aggressive protection and management programs, and to provide wildlife resources and safe watercraft and off-highway vehicle recreation for the enjoyment,

MERLIN D. TUTTLE

appreciation, and use by present and future generations," cannot be achieved without the support of Arizonans, not only the hunters, anglers, and environmentalists, but all the citizens of our state. Keep that in mind as you read on. Meanwhile, ponder the reality that what is described in this book is still out there for you to enjoy, whether deep in the wilderness, in your backyard, or vicariously from the comfort of your armchair.

How you enjoy Arizona's wildlife is your choice, and the spectrum of choices is as broad as the spectrum of wildlife we enjoy. The Arizona Game and Fish Department will work to safeguard your choices, so you and your successors will continue to have them to make. A hundred years from now, someone will be able to objectively measure our success in this work. Until then the jury is out, but early returns indicate that we, and Arizona's wonderful wildlife legacy, are doing all right. After reading this book, maybe you'll drop us a line and tell us what you think.

Birds
of
Arizona

Great blue heron
Photo by Aimee Madsen

Arizona is famous for many things, but short of the Grand Canyon perhaps for no aspect of its natural history as much as for its birdlife. The official state bird list, maintained by the Arizona Bird Committee, now numbers about 519 species. The list includes a number of casual and vagrant species, including birds that have occurred here only as wind-blown waifs, that may not reasonably be expected to occur here again. But it also includes about 275 species that breed here regularly and another 100 or more that are regular visitors in winter or during spring or autumn migration. That is quite an avifauna, one that is rivaled only by those of California, Texas, and Florida for the mainland United States. Best of all, it includes only a few species that are not native, but which have become established after introduction by humans.

The topography and location of Arizona combine to make its avifauna so rich. Elevation here ranges from 70 feet above sea level near Yuma to more than 12,000 feet in the San Francisco Peaks, near Flagstaff. Our landscape includes wildlife elements of the Rocky Mountains, Great Plains, Mexican Sierra Madres, and all four North American deserts — the Great Basin, Mohave, Chihuahuan, and Sonoran. And, although Arizona has no true beachfront property, our rivers, man-made lakes and playas attract thousands of shorebirds and other species that we typically think of as coastal birds.

The birds of Arizona have been the subject of many a book, several excellent field guides, and innumerable magazine articles. This special edition of Arizona Wildlife Views is not intended to replace any of them, but rather as a handy introductory guide to encourage people to take a second look at birds and birdwatching, perhaps for the first time. All things considered, if Arizona is not birding heaven, it must be very close. So we hope that you enjoy what the state's birdwatching has to offer, and what we have to say and show you about it.

Text for this special Wildlife Views Birding Issue by Terry B. Johnson
Design by Roberta Dobolek

Vermilion flycatcher. *Photo by Robert Campbell*

Waterfowl

GEORGE ANDREJKO

American Wigeon

The bold white stripe on the male's head, set off below by a vivid green stripe, causes this bird to be called "baldpate." By any name, it is a migrant and wintering bird in Arizona. With the exception of urban lakes, it is rarely seen in large numbers anywhere in the state. The American wigeon is most commonly encountered mixed with a variety of other waterfowl in rafts on open, often shallow, waters. In flight, the large white patches on the upper wings, and the white axillary (armpit) feathers, help distinguish this species. An Old World cousin, the European wigeon also occasionally visits the West, and has included Arizona in its wide-ranging travels.

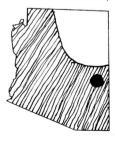

Many people are first exposed to birdwatching as children, when their parents take them to the park to observe ducks and geese. It is often a pleasant experience, that builds memories that last a lifetime. Although some of the waterfowl seen in those settings are domesticated and do not occur in the wild, most park menageries include at least a few wild birds that have found some kindred spirits with which to rest awhile. Picking out the wild ones can be a rewarding experience for the birder, as sometimes very rare species show up in very mundane settings. Serendipity is part and parcel of birdwatching.

At least 34 species of waterfowl have been recorded in Arizona. They include resident breeding birds, such as cinnamon and green-winged teal, and wintering species, such as northern shovelers and canvasback. Three species of the slightly strange-looking mergansers — hooded, common, and red-breasted — occur in Arizona. Our larger waterfowl include breeding Canada geese, and wintering or migrating tundra swans. Among our more unusual species, some of which have been reported just a few times, are the Eurasian wigeon, oldsquaw, and Barrow's goldeneye. And despite their generally coastal and northern occurrence, all three North American scoters have been recorded in Arizona — the black, surf, and white-winged.

Many of Arizona's breeding ducks occur in the few marshlands that remain from historical times. The Department has an active marshland restoration project underway to expand the habitat these species require. The project is funded by an Arizona Waterfowl Stamp, and is supplemented by allocations from private conservation groups, such as Ducks Unlimited, and a great deal of matching monies from Heritage lottery funds. Even people who don't hunt sometimes buy the waterfowl stamp, just to support marshland conservation efforts that aid many nonwaterfowl species, from waterbirds to shorebirds to marsh wrens and blackbirds.

Other species of native waterfowl make effective use of man-made lakes along the Colorado, Salt, Gila, and other rivers, or those in the highlands, as in the White Mountains and on the Coconino and Kaibab plateaus. Some species use the rivers themselves, but the rafts of ducks on lakes Mead and Powell, or in the generating pools below most any mainstream Colorado River dam, can be especially impressive. Streams, river backwaters, and artesian- or rain-fed stock ponds also offer resting or breeding habitat for waterfowl here. In a desert land, no water can be wasted, by man or beast.

JUDD COONEY

Blue-winged Teal

A common sight during migration on marshes and small lakes and ponds throughout Arizona, the blue-winged teal is a pretty, if small, package of feathers. Each year the blue-wing is among the earliest migrant waterfowl arriving in Arizona. The white quarter-moon in front of the male's eye, and matched by a splash of white at the rear end, is distinctive. But for most birdwatchers, and all casual observers, female blue-wings are best identi-fied by—presence of the males. Blue-wings may breed occasionally in several places in Arizona's Rim Country and in the southern part of the state, but are usually seen in that season as very isolated pairs.

Canada Goose

Of all the geese that occur in western North America, this is the one that deserves the name "honker." The characteristic v-shaped flights of these large, tasty birds are well known to most people who set foot in the wild, and to everyone who watches their wildlife from the comfort of an arm-chair set before a television. Even so, many people are surprised to learn that Canada geese breed in several localities in Arizona, mainly in the high country, but also including a few low elevation sites, such as Roosevelt Lake. Wherever they go, Canada geese are easily recognized by a distinctive white chin strap, which is set off by a black head and neck.

MEL SARGENT

Cinnamon Teal

The amazingly bright, rich breeding plumage of the male cinnamon teal, contrasted by a blue wing patch that any blue-winged teal would envy, is probably the envy of the waterfowl world. It more than makes up for the drab female, which is easily mistaken by anyone except the male cinnamon as a blue-winged teal. Cinnamon teal are most com-mon on smaller lakes and ponds in Arizona, and are usually seen in small numbers at any one site in any season. The most common breeding sites in this state are in the high country, but several low desert lakes, marshes, and river backwaters also help pro-duce cinnamons.

STEVEN W. SMITH

KEVIN ELLIS

Hooded Merganser

If you didn't know this bird existed, you would likely question your eyesight on first encountering it. Not very commonly seen in Arizona, hooded mergansers most often appear here as singletons or in small groups along the lower Colorado River and in the southern part of the state. The boldly marked male, with a puffy rounded crest, is quite a sight. The female suffers a bit from the "just-another-drab-brown-duck" syndrome, but on careful inspection it is also seen as finely feathered. Like all mergansers, the hooded's serrated bill is well adapted for catching the small fish that are the mainstay of its diet. The fish, aquatic crustaceans, and other prey are most often taken during dives.

Mallard

Many of the ducks of barnyards and urban lakes are domesticated or lazy mallards that have adjusted to the bizarre existence of life on a popcorn and white-bread diet. They bear little behavioral, and sometimes not too much physical, resemblance to the wild mallards that visit such settings in the winter. The green-headed male and the drab brown female mallard are also frequently seen in their natural (or man-made) breeding habitat in this state, the marshes and lakes of central and northern Arizona, and along the lower Colorado River. The wild mallards of southeastern Arizona's potholes and marshes were once known as Mexican ducks, and for many years were considered a separate species. Male "Mexican ducks" have a basically female mallard plumage.

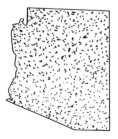

JUDD COONEY

Northern Pintail

Perhaps the most elegant waterfowl in all of North America, the pintail is simply regal. There are probably prettier ducks, and certainly gaudier and more brightly colored ducks, but there are no ducks that seem as royal as the pintail. Oh, the gracefully curved, slender neck, marked on the male by a projection of the white body color, and with a sweeping pointed tail as a perfect counterpoint. Sometimes including hundreds of individuals, rafts of wintering and migrating pintails are a sight to behold. They are most often seen on open waters and larger impoundments, but even a small marsh or a sewage pond may occasionally have this touch of avian elegance.

Redhead

Just like Charlie Brown is always aware of the red-haired girl, waterfowlers are always looking for the redhead. Small wonder. A rather compact looking duck, with a distinctly rounded head and short neck, even at a distance the redhead can easily be told from most any other waterfowl. The short blue bill, with a black tip and a white ring separating the black from the blue, and a much smaller body size, help distinguish the redhead from the canvasback, which has a similar plumage pattern. Redheads may be less common now than 20 years ago, but they are every bit as memorable. Their wintering presence in Arizona is well appreciated.

Ring-necked Duck

The ring-necked duck, recognized by most people by the bold white ring on its bill, is a frequent sight on open waters and in marshes throughout Arizona in the winter. Bigger than a teal, but smaller than the most heavily hunted ducks, it also nests here, principally in the White Mountain region. The male's purple head, black chest and dark back set off by pale sides are quite distinctive. If lesser or greater scaup are in the area, then it's time to look again for the ringed bill that does not give this bird its name.

GEORGE ANDREJKO

GEORGE ANDREJKO

GEORGE ANDREJKO

PAT O'BRIEN

Snow Goose

Decades ago, snow geese were abundant in winter along the lower Colorado River. Now they occur there in just a few spots, and usually in numbers that are all too easily counted. Little more than half the size of a big Canada goose, this remarkably white bird has black-wing tips and, painted on its pink bill, a black "grinning patch" that gives it a permanent smile. Snow geese are probably seen more often flying to or feeding in agricultural fields (a habit that is not uniformly appreciated by all humans) than sitting on water. The very similar Ross' goose also occurs in Arizona occasionally, but it lacks the grinning patch of the snow.

Wood Duck

With a crest resembling that of a merganser, and a brightly colored head and body resembling no other native waterfowl, the male wood duck is not likely to be confused with any other bird. Even the female has a very distinctive pale teardrop running back from the eye that sets it apart from all the other more or less drab brown females of the waterfowl world. Too bad this hole-nesting species isn't more common in parts of Arizona that are frequently visited by most people. As it is, your best chance to see this species is often at sewage treatment plants in several urban settings. Even there, wood ducks usually occur as pairs or in very small groups.

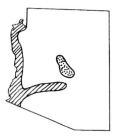

JUDD COONEY

Waterbirds

A s evidenced by our waterfowl, no puddle of water in Arizona is too small to support birds. Actually, sometimes all it takes is a bit of mud to draw a crowd. But there are indeed many species of water-oriented birds here that are not ducks or geese. In fact, the vast majority of our waterbirds are from orders other than Anseriformes, the one which includes all waterfowl.

It may seem strange, but Arizona's waterbirds begin with species that we think of as birds of the frozen north. Four species of loons have visited our state, and two of them are rather common as wintering birds or migrants. Loons are ungainly at best on land, as their legs are positioned at the very rear of their portly bodies. But these birds are aquatic acrobats of the highest order, diving to depths of hundreds of feet (well, not very often in Arizona) as they chase—and catch—fish. The haunting yodel of a courting loon may not be heard often under the desert sun, but seeing one of these birds always brings it to mind.

Grebes, cormorants, pelicans, and a host of oceanic type birds also call Arizona home, or at least visit here occasionally. Some of these birds are literally blown into the state on the gale winds of Pacific storms that sweep in from California and the west coast of Mexico. A few simply seem to fly up the Gulf of California and fail to recognize the International Border, continuing up the Colorado River to the various impoundments and marshlands below Lake Mead. If you've never heard of, let alone seen, a blue-footed booby or a magnificent frigatebird, today in Arizona may be your lucky day. If not, maybe tomorrow.

Herons, egrets, and all kinds of wading birds frequent our lakes, rivers, playas, and marshes. Rails and moorhens skulk about in the reeds and cattails, and occasionally come into view, usually just long enough to whet your appetite for a real look. At times some places along the lower Colorado River look like the Florida Everglades, with flocks of large wading birds moving from rookeries to foraging grounds. In winter, these groups may include thousands of sandhill cranes, as well as countless waterfowl. And even a casual look along the shallows and on the mudflats may reveal hundreds of wintering or migrating shorebirds, including all kinds of unidentifiable sandpipers, plovers and their relatives. In an Arizona marshland, especially at low elevation, during migration the bird overhead is as likely to be a gull or a tern as it is a swallow. Well, almost.

American Bittern

JUDD COONEY

Oonk-a-tsoonk, oonk-a-tsoonk, oonk-a-tsoonk. The deep, haunting call of the "thunder pumper" rolls across the marsh at night, throughout the spring and summer. The American, the larger of the two bitterns in Arizona, inhabits marshlands and very wet meadows along rivers, lakes, and ponds. It is rarely seen away from dense reeds, cattails, and other emergent vegetation. Arizona's few breeding birds are now largely confined to the Colorado River, although occasionally summering birds are reported from a few high country localities. American bitterns are masters at stalking, but also at still hunting. Poised motionless at the water's edge, they suddenly thrust their bills forward to seize fish, frog, or snake. Availability more than preference dictates the diet of this rather non-selective predator.

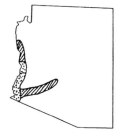

JUDD COONEY

GEORGE ANDREJKO

GEORGE ANDREJKO

American Coot

Though not a duck at all, the American coot is known by that name to many children. It is in fact more closely related to rails and gallinules than to waterfowl. Regardless of taxonomy, even more people know it and dismiss it as "just a darn mudhen." It's too common and widespread for birdwatchers to value and too bad tasting for hunters to pursue. Perhaps a little more attention is warranted, though, because few species offer better opportunities to observe the full range of animal behavior. Most lakes and ponds in Arizona have a full complement of coots. Try watching these birds scampering about in courtship displays and aggressive interactions, and diving for food. It's not unlike watching a "Three Stooges" movie.

Black-necked Stilt

Like a piece of fine china, black-necked stilts are exquisitely painted and oh so delicate. All day long, they prance about in shallow fresh or brackish waters and on mud flats, in search of invertebrates that are usually too small to see from even a very close vantage point. Known mainly as a common migrant in southern and western Arizona, black-necked stilts also breed here, principally along the lower Colorado River. The sharply contrasting black and white pattern, the long thin bill, and the coral legs make this species absolutely, positively unmistakable, by anyone, young or old. Now how many birds can you say that about and not be lying?

Common Moorhen

Another bird of well developed marshlands with expanses of emergent vegetation, the moorhen is a fairly common but local resident in southern and western Arizona. It also occurs in smaller patches of cattails and reeds, as sometimes occur along irrigation canals — especially those that are not well maintained. On first glance, casual observers may dismiss individuals of this species as American coots, or mudhens. But a closer look will reveal significant differences in body, bill, and leg color and shape. Either species may be seen picking its way through the emergent vegetation, but the moorhen seems to step a little more confidently and lightly. Also, the moorhen definitely does not stray as far from vegetation while swimming as coots do.

PAT O'BRIEN

Common Snipe

The common snipe is a pretty bird, but in truth it is more fun to "watch" when you can't see it. On the breeding grounds, which in Arizona means basically the Springerville area, the snipe performs a courtship display at night that is a sight for sore ears. Flying over the wet meadows and marshes in which it nests, the male makes erratic dives during which its specialized tail feathers vibrate, producing a strange, somewhat eerie, fluttering sound. The display must work, because these birds are prolific. During the day, snipes sit tight, even when approached closely. At the last possible instant, they explode into flight, zig-zagging wildly in the evasive pattern that jet fighters emulate in combat.

Cormorants

Arizona has two species of cormorants. The smaller one, the neotropic, occurs in the southcentral and southeastern part of the state, such as at Lake Patagonia State Park and at stock ponds and various other waters. The other, the double-crested, occurs throughout much of the state as a transient, as a wintering bird, and, especially along the lower Colorado River, as a breeding bird. It frequents large lakes as well as the rivers, but it also shows up at smaller waters. Both species are fish eaters. OK, now get your field guides out.

NED SMITH

Range map shown is for double-crested cormorant only.

Godwits & Willets

When the creator made peeps, He also made godwits and willets so novice birdwatchers would have at least a few species of shorebirds they could identify relatively easily by sight or by sound, thus impressing their families with their remarkable acuity. Both species occur in Arizona as migrants only, though out-of-season records exist for both. Marbled godwits are most common along the lower Colorado River. Willets occur there too, but also including even northeastern Arizona in their travels. Both species can often be observed closely and at your leisure, as they rest or forage along the water's edge and on exposed mud flats.

DAVE DAUGHTRY

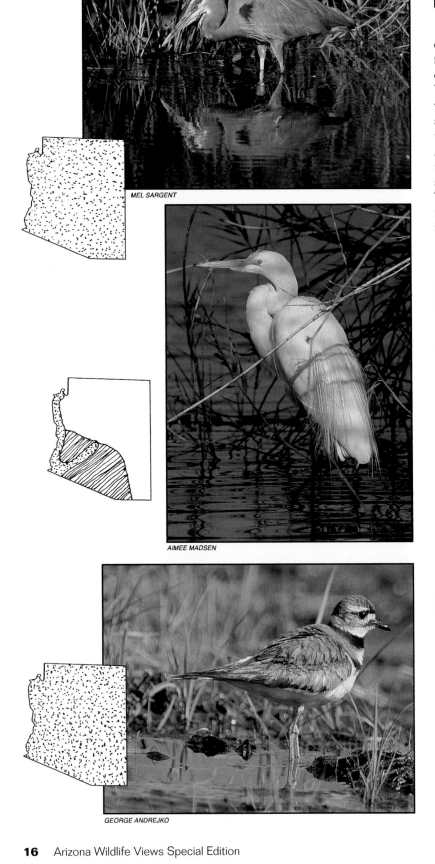

MEL SARGENT

AIMEE MADSEN

GEORGE ANDREJKO

Great Blue Heron

This, the largest of our herons, is a gangly but common sight at almost any permanent water, flowing or not, in Arizona, but especially in the central, southern, and western parts of the state. With a hearty *gronnkk*, the great blue takes flight when approached. Flapping its wings heavily, like a human trying to fly, the big bird eventually picks up speed and then moves along at a very strong clip. As soon as the threat disappears, the bird returns to the water's edge to stalk fish and frogs, or most anything it can spear with a lightning thrust of its bill. The huge nests this species builds are easily seen in tall remnant trees that remind us of riparian gallery forests that once were, and may some day be again.

Great Egret

A little smaller than the great blue heron, the great egret is roughly twice the size of the other two white heron relatives in Arizona, the cattle egret and snowy egret. A combination of a yellow bill and black legs also separate it from the other white egrets. Like most of these other big wading birds, the great egret is most common as a breeding bird in the lower Colorado Valley. However, small nesting colonies also occur along most other permanent, low-elevation waterways that have marshlands dominated by cattails and other emergent vegetation. Like the other waders, it carefully, patiently stalks a variety of aquatic prey. The great egret favors fairly open areas for its foraging activities.

Killdeer

The distraction display of the killdeer is well known to urban dwellers and rural residents alike. Most of us have swallowed the bait, and have tried to walk up on a seemingly injured bird that is dragging its wing, only to have it finally take flight and leave us a hundred yards from where we started, and from where its nest is. The killdeer is an adaptable cuss. It occurs along virtually every lower-elevation water course, in irrigated fields, on lake shores, and on golf courses. Year-round residents, killdeers are simply ubiquitous and common — and clever.

Least Bittern

Half the size of and perhaps more common than an American bittern, this secretive little bird also haunts dense marshes and is rarely seen unless it flushes. Then the bold buffy wing patches are exposed, and instantly identify the fleeing creature. Least bitterns are resident along the lower Colorado Valley, and in the few well developed marshes in central Arizona. Transient and wintering birds are of course more widely dispersed, and somewhat erratic in occurrence. Like its larger relative, when alarmed, if the least bittern does not flush, it tends to freeze in place, with its bill pointed to the sky. The streaked neck is thus exposed fully, allowing the bird to blend even more closely with the marsh vegetation.

WES KEYES

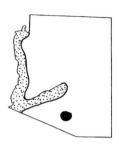

Long-billed Dowitcher

If you've ever had a chance to watch dowitchers in action, you know why they are called "sewing machines." It's not because these gregarious birds have a predilection for sleeping away the day. During their waking minutes, dowitchers sometimes forage in water that is so deep it appears as if the birds must be swimming rather than wading. All the while, their heads bob up and down in high-speed sewing machine fashion as their long bills probe the mud for invertebrates. Actually two species of dowitchers occur in Arizona, and neither species breeds here. The other species, the short-billed dowitcher, is much less common with most records in southern and western Arizona. Even very experienced birdwatchers find it challenging to identify these two species confidently *and* correctly.

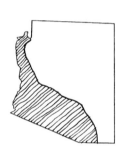

JOHN H. HOFFMAN

Pelicans

White and brown pelicans both occur in Arizona, and either may turn up just about anywhere. The former is a regular migrant here, but also winters and sometimes summers (but does not breed) along the lower Colorado River. In contrast, the brown pelican usually shows up here in the summer or autumn, and often in dire straits. Browns tend to get confused by heat ripples on highways, and, apparently thinking the mirages will slake their thirst, they dive into the concrete or asphalt. If they survive the sudden stop, they sometimes cannot take flight again. The Department ships a dozen or more of these rescued birds to California each year, for rehabilitation at Sea World before release into an area with real water. And, truly, for each species, the beak can indeed hold more than the belly can.

GEORGE ANDREJKO

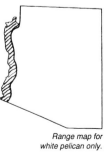

Range map for white pelican only.

MEL SARGENT

MIKE PELLEGATTI

JUDD COONEY

Sandhill Crane

Of all the birding sights in Arizona, and there are countless to appreciate, none is more spectacular than the flights of thousands of wintering sandhill cranes in the Willcox Playa. At daylight, moving from night roosts in the Playa to agricultural lands scattered across the Sulphur Springs valley, these large birds stretch their necks out as they power their way through the sky. Their loud rolling rattle, *garrooooooo garrooooooo*, can be heard a mile away. The evening flights back to the roosting area are also worth watching, but tend to take place over a longer period and are thus somewhat less spectaular. Smaller numbers of sandhills also winter along the lower Colorado River.

Sandpipers

Sandpipers are proof the almighty has a sense of humor. Why else would so many species be similar enough to make birders fight over whether a little blob 200 feet away has blackish or mud-stained yellowish-green legs? Imagine a mud flat with 1,000 birds, asleep with heads tucked beneath wings, or scampering about too quickly to follow with a scope. Are they the same species, or ten? It's almost enough to make me take up bowling. But then I stumble across one that is bigger than a peep, too small for a yellowlegs, doesn't bob like a spotted, and lacks the white rump of a stilt sandpiper. It's a solitary sandpiper. Isn't it? Please let it be. I *need* it to be!

White-faced Ibis

In breeding plumage, there is not much doubt about what separates this species from its close relative, the glossy ibis. The reddish face, bordered in white, and the red decurved bill and red legs must be seen, preferably through a 20 power spotting scope, to be believed. Seen in strong sunlight, the rich chestnut body and oily almost iridescent green and purple wings make this wader as beautiful as any bird in North America. White-faced ibises are not at all predictable in Arizona. They are likely to be seen at almost any wetland or sewage treatment facility in migration, but their presence is always a very pleasant surprise. The icing on the cake is the fact that, often, when you find one, you find a dozen or more.

Ground Birds

JUDD COONEY

Penguins aside, feathers and flight are what make birds birds. When people think of birds, they generally think of something singing or flying. Yet there are many birds that are principally ground dwelling. In some regions of the world, these birds include flightless, or poorly flighted species, such as ostriches (Africa), rheas (South America), and emus (Australia). Bird scientists, technically known as ornithologists, know these species as the "ratites," birds that lack a well-developed keel on the sternum (breast bone) to which chest muscles can attach. Since strong chest muscles are essential to flight, the terrestrial nature of these species is understandable.

There are many ground-dwelling birds around the world other than ratites. The secretarybird of Africa, tinamous in South America, the kiwi in New Zealand, etc. Some of these species can fly very well, others fly rather poorly and tire very quickly, returning to earth as quickly as possible when forced to fly.

Arizona has a few species that fit this decidedly non-scientific, layman's classification scheme, which focuses on mode of life rather than on the evolutionary relationships and morphological, cellular and physiological traits that thrill the dedicated ornithologist. Many of them are game birds, species that have populations sufficiently large to withstand a carefully regulated harvest. These include species such as the wild turkey, the nonnative ring-necked pheasant, quail (Arizona has three widely-occurring native species, plus the recently reintroduced masked bobwhite and a couple of introduced species), and the blue grouse and its introduced relative from the Old World, the chukar.

The greater roadrunner, the American Southwest's version of the African secretarybird, is also included with the ground-dwelling species in this section. And for convenience, we have also included the white-winged dove. Not because it is incapable of flight or even poorly flighted. Certainly it is anything but either of those. But like the roadrunner and many game birds, most doves spend a lot of their time foraging on the ground, searching for seeds and for grit to help grind the seeds as they pass through the digestive tract.

Since the white-winged dove was included with these species, another member of the same family, the band-tailed pigeon, was also included. Which illustrates how easy it is to begin with a reasonably logical thought process and, through allowing a sequence of slightly but ever broader interpretations, end up with a rather illogical component. You see, just about the last thing that comes to mind when you think of a strong-flying mountain dwelling band-tailed pigeon is ground-dwelling.

Band-tailed Pigeon

Look for band-tails in the oak woodlands and along wooded middle-elevation water courses of southeastern and central to northern Arizona. They also nest in lower conifer forests, but it is in the acorn belt that they thrive. At first glance, these relatively large birds may seem like just another flock of urban pigeons (which are actually rock doves), but with a second look you may note the conspicuous slash of white on the nape, and the tail band that gives the species its name. The call of this rather easily overlooked bird is a very low *whoo-whoo* that can be a bit difficult to locate.

KEVIN ELLIS

Blue Grouse

If you are looking for a blue grouse in Arizona, perhaps the best place to search is in the White Mountains on the trail up Mount Baldy, above Phelps Cabin. On a late summer day, with the wildflowers blooming in the meadows of the conifer forest and the air beginning to show signs of the crisp autumn days that will soon follow, you will probably never care if you don't find the bird you seek. Which is good, because the odds are you won't find it. Unless you stumble across these birds while they putter about foraging, or find a male hooting and strutting about in its elaborate spring-time courtship display, they are most likely to slip quietly off into the woods before you are aware of their presence.

JUDD COONEY

Chukar

From the wilds of the Old World, the chukar was brought to the Old West as a highly prized game species. It favors relatively dry, rocky, mountainous areas. The small coveys can be found, but not without persistence and considerable physical effort. As with many game birds, chukars occasionally turn up in Phoenix and Tucson, when they escape from aviculturists. However, Arizona's major wild populations are on the North Rim of the Grand Canyon and on the Kaibab Plateau. The birds there actually stem from wild-trapped stock that was transplanted from California and Nevada in the late 1950s.

PAT O'BRIEN

Gambel's Quail

Strutting through the desertscrub, the Gambel's quail is, to many tourists, *the* wildlife symbol of Arizona. A splash of color here and there, just enough to break up the monotony but not too much to make it easy to hide from the many predators that pursue this sassy bird throughout the year. Good winter rains and crops of spring annuals yield an abundance of Gambel's quail, as can easily be measured on encountering the broods of a half dozen to a dozen or more chicks. The precocial youngsters scatter wildly at any intrusion, but quickly reassemble when the sentinel male gives the "all clear" signal.

Greater Roadrunner

One of the few legends that lives up to its billing, though not confined to the Sonoran Desert, the roadrunner is as much at home here as any beast. Not satisfied with the mid-day sun of the proverbial "hot stinking desert," the roadrunner gets a head start on the heat by raising the feathers on its back to reveal a dark skin patch that absorbs the early morning rays and gets its body temperature up to a level suitable for frenetic behavior that at times does seem cartoon-like. And this relative of the cuckoo actually does hunt snakes, even rattlers. Successfully, too! Lizards, rodents, birds, in fact almost anything small that walks or crawls is fair game for this voracious predator.

MEL SARGENT

Montezuma Quail

The bird with as many names as a bad-check artist. Whether called Mearns' quail, Harlequin quail, fool's quail, or its currently correct name, Montezuma quail, this species is among the most elusive prey of visiting birdwatchers. It is unsurpassed in its ability to sit tight in the grass as people walk past. The painted face of the male is unmistakable, and a remarkable counterpoint to the earthen tones of the female. After the summer rains begin in southern Arizona, stop along a grassy arroyo in the lower oaks and juniper woodlands and listen for the distinctive, soft whinnying whistle of this elusive bird. If you try listening from an hour or so before to just after sunrise, you might hear it.

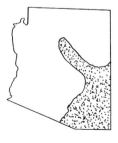

JUDD COONEY

PAT O'BRIEN

JOHN H. HOFFMAN

GERRY BLAIR

Ring-necked Pheasant

Though it is not native to Arizona, many attempts have been made to establish the ring-necked pheasant in several areas of the state. Most of the introductions have been on private hunting preserves, but some aviculturists have accidentally contributed to the cause by allowing captive birds to escape. Look for ring-necks in the Verde Valley, and in semidesert grasslands north and south of Tucson and near Safford. They also turn up occasionally in various neighborhoods in Phoenix and Tucson. The long, pointed tail of this stubby-winged native Asian bird makes it unlikely to be confused with any other Arizona species, though with some effort and imagination it can be made into a greater roadrunner.

White-winged Dove

The white-winged dove's colonial nests were once too abundant in Arizona to count, but the riparian forests and woodlands in which they occurred are largely gone now. Fortunately, the resounding "Who cooks for you?" chorus of this fast but graceful flier is still among the more conspicuous spring and early summer sounds of central and southern Arizona. White-wings flashing in the sunlight are a common sight as they fly from scattered nests to their favorite, often distant, feeding and watering spots. And who among us would not recognize the profile of a white-wing perched atop a saguaro, feeding at the flowers and fruit that spring forth in May and June?

Wild Turkey

It's easy to see why Ben Franklin preferred this bird as America's symbol. The wild turkey is as smart as the male is gaudy. Matching wits with this bird is no easy task, for birdwatcher or hunter. No other Arizona bird is more watchable, or seems as shy. Even the unmistakable loud call of the male may not be enough to pin down the whereabouts of this wily bird in its mountain forest and woodland home. To find flocks and young, look in the oaks in the autumn. Spring is best for looking, or listening, for toms (males), as they strut about and utter that unmistakable gobble-gobble-gobble before adoring hens.

Raptors

W hen defining which birds are raptors, or birds of prey, it is pretty straight-forward what structural and behavioral traits are being considered. Raptorial birds generally have strongly hooked beaks, sharp claws or even talons, and by definition they feed on other animals. But as with anything else, it sometimes isn't exactly clear where you draw the line.

Purists probably consider raptors to include only the vultures, osprey, falcons, hawks, eagles, and owls. These species represent only two of the 30 orders of living birds, Falconiformes and Strigiformes. Clearly there are other predatory species to be considered. Thus, some discussions of raptors would include such species as crows and their close relatives, ravens and jays. Others would go a step farther and include such species as shrikes, the butcher birds that impale their small prey on thorns and barbed wire, for future use. But, since Arizona has an abundance of truly raptorial species of falcons, hawks and owls, we have not included those other, borderline species in this section.

Arizona's avifauna includes 2 species of vultures, the osprey, 2 kites, 2 eagles, 15 hawks, the crested caracara, 4 falcons and 13 owls. Add to these 40 species the California condor and the aplomado falcon, both of which occurred here historically, and you have a total of 42 species for the state (the snowy owl is too poorly documented to date to include as a bona fide Arizonan).

In remarkable contrast to most game birds, many raptors have relatively small populations. In fact, a few have such small and threatened populations that those species are listed under the federal Endangered Species Act, or are included in the Department's list of *Wildlife of Special Concern in Arizona*. Among these are the southwestern bald eagle and the aplomado falcon. Several other species seem to be similarly imperiled, and are candidates for federal listing. These include the Mexican spotted owl and the northern goshawk.

Given their position at the top of the food chain, raptors are generally good indicators of the over-all health of ecosystems. Problems at lower levels in the chain are multiplied by the time they are exhibited at the top. Body-fat concentrations of DDT and other organochlorine pesticides are good examples of this problem. Thus carefully monitoring raptor populations can be an essential component of a state conservation program, and tip us off to problems that must be addressed if we are to leave our successors a natural heritage at least as good as the one we received from our forefathers.

JOHN H. HOFFMAN

American Kestrel

The kestrel is the elf owl analog of the falcons of North America. At 10 inches total length, this species seems like no match for anything bigger than a decent sized sparrow or a large grasshopper. In truth, those are among the principal prey items of this species, but kestrels will defend their cavity nests against virtually any intruder, and occasionally can be seen putting all discretion aside and harassing red-tailed hawks and other large raptors, apparently just for the fun of it. Kestrels migrate through and breed virtually throughout Arizona, and winter here almost as widely. But in winter, the sexes divide the habitats pretty cleanly, with the slightly larger females holding on to the better territories.

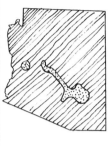

KEVIN ELLIS

Bald Eagle

Arizona is home to about 40 breeding pairs of bald eagles, but in winter the numbers may reach 200 to 300 birds. When the northern winter is harsh, and lakes freeze over, more eagles fly south in search of waterfowl and fish, their principal prey. Our nesting birds occur at lower elevations, mainly in the Gila, Salt, and Verde river watersheds, but in winter or migration bald eagles may be seen almost anywhere in the state. Twenty or more of these great birds are occasionally seen at some favorite roosting or foraging site in winter or spring. The bald eagle is a part of our heritage that virtually everyone agrees is well worth protecting, and which everyone is thrilled on seeing.

BILL GIRDEN

Cooper's Hawk

The legendary chicken hawk, in the flesh, or in the feather. A medium-sized accipiter, the Cooper's hawk is built for speed and definitely for catching birds. But, truthfully, chickens are not among its principal prey items. This avian specialist occurs widely through Arizona, breeding in the deserts as well as in the mountains. Unlike its close relative, the goshawk, this species tolerates a much more open forest and a wider variety of habitats. Resident birds are joined in winter by their northerly counterparts, which find Arizona's climate and abundant "snowbird" population much more to their liking.

JUDD COONEY

Crested Caracara

With a large head, long legs, long neck and a very heavy bill, the crested caracara is very distinctive—enough so that is also called the Mexican eagle. Indeed it is the national bird for Mexico. Add a blood red fleshy base to the bill and there is no chance to confuse this consummate roadside scavenger with any other raptor in Arizona. Occurring principally in the low desert southwest of Tucson, the caracara is most often seen there perched atop a saguaro. It preys on live rodents and large insects occasionally, but carrion is its mainstay. Only a very few nests are known for this species, which has never been common in Arizona and may well be even less so now.

Elf Owl

Every group has to have its smallest species, and this one accomplishes just that for the owls of North America. Little more than five inches high, the elf owl stands tall at the entrance to its nesting or roosting cavity in a saguaro or low desert to middle-elevation riparian tree. A few individuals are world famous, such as the telephone-pole nesting elf owl at Madera Canyon, in the Santa Rita Mountains of southern Arizona. In contrast to its slightly larger cousins, the pygmy-owls, this species is strictly nocturnal, and its diet is adjusted accordingly. Various invertebrates, very small snakes, and the occasional small rodent are its main diet.

DAVID W. LAZAROFF

Golden Eagle

As large as, or even slightly larger than, the bald eagle, the golden eagle is an entirely different beast. It nests in high places, on the cliffs and crags of Arizona's rugged mountains, virtually statewide. Then, according to Tennyson, it drops like a thunderbolt, usually to take its prey. And surely no jackrabbits are ever more surprised than those that are seized — just once — in the talons of this incredibly powerful bird. Carrion is also an important part of its diet. The golden mantle of the adult bird is typical, but the distinct white at the base of the flight feathers and tail of the immature may cause some confusion with young bald eagles.

MICHAEL MAURO

PAT O'BRIEN

Gray Hawk

There may be as many as 70 pairs of gray hawks along southern Arizona's riparian forests and woodlands, but that's not enough. Perhaps the most beautiful of all our raptors, the adult gray hawk is a sight to behold and a major tourist attraction. Birdwatchers literally flock from around the world to see this species. The few remaining forested segments of the San Pedro and Santa Cruz rivers and their major tributaries are the stonghold for this species now. Agile enough to pick large spiny lizards from mesquites and other trees, it also takes frogs, snakes, and some rodents. Its flight is more like that of an accipiter than of a buteo, the group to which the species belongs.

Great Horned Owl

ROBERT CAMPBELL

Among the most commonly heard noises of the Arizona night, or early morning, is the resonant, but insistent, "who—who—who" of the great horned owl. On feathers softer than silk, these birds patrol their hunting grounds. The flight is silent, but strong. Feet tipped with razor-sharp talons bring a quick end to their prey, whether it be a rodent, rabbit, or a skunk. Territories are established in winter; the young fledge from late winter through spring, depending in part on the weather and the food supply. Great horned owls are as likely to nest atop an urban palm tree or building as on a rocky ledge of a mountain or in a saguaro crotch.

Harris's Hawk

BILL GIRDEN

Also known as the bay winged hawk, a most appropriate name, the Harris's hawk is a familiar sight to Tucson and Phoenix-area residents in the saguaro-paloverde and ironwood belt. Watch for the distinctive white rump and tailbase as you drive through these areas. Living in small communal groups, in which young birds help their parents raise more young for several years before setting off on their own, these raptors hunt cooperatively and very successfully. Sometimes they even pursue their rabbit or packrat prey on the ground, into the Sonoran Desert version of the proverbial briar patch. The keen hunting skills, beauty and adaptable nature of this species have also made it a favorite as a falconry bird.

Mexican Spotted Owl

Like its northerly relative, the Mexican spotted owl is mainly a bird of the ancient coniferous forests, in which dense canopies ensure a cool, moist environment. Some individuals also occur in, and a few even breed successfully in, drier, more open forests and woodlands, but it is the old growth forest that keeps these marvelous birds from extinction. A bit smaller than a great horned owl, this nocturnal species is very different behaviorally. It has the same mammalian focus in prey, but it is so unwary that individuals have been known to fly down and take a mouse from the hand of a biologist who is studying them. A great horned might well try to take the hand and leave the mouse.

BOB MILES

Northern Pygmy-owl

This rather common but tiny owl is well worth noting. Resident in conifer forests throughout most of mountainous Arizona, the northern pygmy-owl also occurs in pine-oak woodlands in the southern part of the state. It is chiefly diurnal, but may be especially active at dawn and dusk. This 6- to 7-inch tall predator makes its living chiefly on small birds. Its repetitive *hoo hoo* is very recognizable, and birdwatchers can whistle these notes to attract forest birds that often mob pygmy-owls. At lower elevations this species is replaced by the cactus ferruginous pygmy-owl, which is now largely restricted to a few saguaro forests, as around Tucson and in Organ Pipe Cactus National Monument.

JOHN LOFGREEN

WES KEYES

Osprey

Ospreys are among Arizona's finest anglers. During migration they may be seen anywhere, but they nest here primarily along streams or rivers in coniferous forests in the White Mountains and across the Mogollon Plateau. A few occur year-round at lower elevations along the Salt and Gila rivers, but no nests have been found there yet. Ospreys hunt from perches near water, but also while hovering or gliding 50 to 100 feet above water. They plunge feet first into the water, sometimes completely submerging, to snatch their prey with long, sharp talons. An ability to lift-off from water while grasping a four-pound fish demonstrates their power. Even so, their food is sometimes stolen in flight by bald eagles, which are much larger birds.

JOHN H. HOFFMAN

Peregrine Falcon

Speed, power, and elegance are the hallmarks of the peregrine falcon. Even while perched, it seems in command, and fast. In fact, there is no faster animal. The peregrine reaches speeds of nearly 200 mph while stooping (plummeting) from on high to take its prey on the wing. Shorebirds, songbirds, waterfowl, and even bats are among this 16- to 21-inch tall bird's typical prey. This species seems well on its way back from the pesticide-induced population crash that began in the 1940s. Arizona may have the largest breeding peregrine population in the 48 contiguous states, with more than 100 occupied aeries (nest sites) confirmed statewide. As in other parts of its almost worldwide range, the nests are typically on ledges on sheer cliff faces that rise a thousand or more feet above the surrounding landscape.

Red-tailed Hawk

The most widespread, common, and taken-for-granted of all of Arizona's birds of prey is unquestionably the red-tailed hawk. Red-tails are everywhere, from the hottest deserts of southwestern Arizona to the conifer clad peaks of the Rim Country and the Sky Islands. And no movie with a western setting is ever shot that does not include the piercing shriek of the red-tail. Even if you don't recognize it for what it is, you've heard the sound a thousand times. Preying mainly on rodents and the occasional jackrabbit, cottontail or road-killed anything, the red-tail is an adaptable survivor and year-round resident.

Swainson's Hawk

With its relatively long, narrow wings canted much like those of a turkey vulture, the Swainson's hawk soars across its Arizona breeding grounds, the semidesert and plains grasslands of the southeastern and northeastern part of the state. It's good practice, too, for the thousands of miles this species will fly each autumn to its wintering grounds in South America, and each spring on the way back north. And all that on a diet composed largely of large insects! The Swainson's hawk is as variable a raptor as there is in North America, with a dark phase and a light phase and all stages in between. The light phase is especially distinctive, though, because in contrast to most raptors, its wing linings are pale and the undersides of the flight feathers are dark.

Turkey Vulture

For a bird that is seen almost statewide from early spring to mid-autumn, it is amazing that so few turkey vulture nests have been found in Arizona. But then, who would want to find one? They are every bit as foul smelling as you would expect for a bird that makes its living scavenging from rotting carcasses of almost anything. Despite its foul and ecologically valuable food habits, the turkey vulture is a pleasure to watch in flight. Teetering on the breezes, effortless floating on thermals and updrafts for hours on end, there is no more accomplished flier in the state. But don't you sometimes get the feeling they are just waiting up there, for you?

MEL SARGENT

GEORGE ANDREJKO

JOHN H. HOFFMAN

Perching

Bell's Vireo

In California, a form of Bell's vireo is endangered, and people keep trying to lump the Arizona populations with those remnant western birds. But as anyone who has visited riparian woodlands and scrub thickets along most any low elevation river, stream or even many dry washes, knows, in Arizona, Bell's vireo is alive and well. And its pleasant and easily recognizable if highly repetitive song, actually a composite of fast, harsh, decidedly nonmusical scolding notes, more than makes up for the relatively nondescript appearance of the bird itself. Almost as active as a ruby-crowned kinglet, Bell's vireo offers some wonderful birdwatching opportunities to recreationists.

JOHN H. HOFFMAN

More than half the birds of the world, and there are about 9021 species known today, are perching birds, members of the Order Passeriformes. In reverse evolutionary sequence, they include the songbirds (oscines) and those that don't sing so well (suboscines). In Arizona, the latter are represented by flycatchers and the former by everything else but the kitchen sink, from jays to thrushes, warblers, sparrows, finches, and orioles.

Simply said, perching birds cover the state. There is no habitat in Arizona, probably no square foot of soil or surface water, nor forest nor grassland, that has not been visited by one of these species, or by their droppings. These are largely the birds that make our picnics memorable, infest our orchards and gardens, and sing their way into our hearts and souls. It is difficult to imagine life without birds, and especially so to imagine life without songbirds, and those perching birds that don't sing too well. After all, we probably shouldn't hold it against a flycatcher if the poor thing can't sing while it swallows all those mosquitoes, flies, and biting gnats. It's far better to put those throat muscles to work in that fashion than to refine them enough to make the syringeal jump to the oscines level.

Perhaps the best way to be overwhelmed by the number of passerine (perching) birds in Arizona is to be in the field on just the right day in spring or fall. The ideal setting is probably an isolated riparian woodland or forest in southern Arizona, but many a montane site will do as well. Migration must be underway, and a major weather front must move in suddenly and impede the flight north (or south). And since the point is to see birds as well as hear them, let's make it happen in early morning. Very early morning. An hour or so before sunrise.

At the drop of a hat, hundreds to thousands of migrant birds begin falling out of the sky, exhausted and hungry or simply too smart to fly into the storm. Flycatchers: we have 25 or so species to choose from. Warblers: we have 40 or more species. Add to those another 20 or so swallows, thrushes, vireos, tanagers, and miscellaneous passerines, as many or more non-perching species, and a host of resident or wintering species, and it's easy to see why a morning in a "migrant trap" can be an exhilarating event. Add a little rain on your field glasses, a chill wind, and it becomes even more challenging, a bit like keeping track of all the honeybees as they leave the hive.

Black-throated Sparrow

The tinkling song and call notes of the black-throated sparrow are among the friendliest sounds of the desert. Often travelling in small flocks, or family groups, black-throats sort of roll across the creosote flats and through the desertscrub, searching for seeds or small invertebrates, depending on season and physiological needs. They tend to forage low in the shrubbery, or on the ground. It's rare if ever that you see these little birds more than four or five feet off the ground. Year-round residents, black-throats occur throughout Arizona at elevations below about the 4,000 to 6,000 foot mark. Once upon a time they were known as desert sparrows, and the name really fits.

JOHN H. HOFFMAN

Black-tailed Gnatcatcher

Of all the desert-dwelling birds in southern Arizona, the black-tailed gnatcatcher is perhaps the most interesting permanent resident. Most often seen along desert washes and in thorny scrub, it is a fascinating bundle of behavior. A tiny, slender bird, the black-tail always seems busy. It builds an elegant little cup-shaped nest, and is as likely to tear it down and rebuild it several times in several places before using it once as it is to go through the "normal" cycle. Foraging pairs maintain close contact, and their scratchy, harsh calls and wheezy song are pleasing to the ear. Two other gnatcatchers occur in Arizona; one is very rare, the other is found at higher elevations and in more mesic situations. But the black-tail is special.

C. ALLAN MORGAN

STEVEN W. SMITH

JUDD COONEY

JOHN H. HOFFMAN

Cactus Wren

The largest of Arizona's seven species of wrens, the cactus wren is also our official State Bird. Somehow it seems very well suited to the position, as it confidently chortles its way through life in the desert. Clambering about in spine-covered shrubs and cacti, searching for termites and other invertebrate delights, it calls loudly, almost incessantly, with that distinctive, low-pitched *chrrg chrrg chrrg chrrg* that sounds disturbingly like every car you've ever had that refused to start. The cactus wren is a friendly sort, clearly a family oriented bird, yet with a no nonsense attitude that implies efficiency and effectiveness. Not a bad choice to represent your state.

Cassin's Finch

Most everyone in Arizona knows this species' close relative, the house finch. In fact, for many people the two species are reasonably indistinguishable. Both have bubbly, persistent, and relatively disorganized songs. Throw in the third member of the group, the purple finch, which is largely a fall-winter visitor here, and many people would throw in the towel. But the house finch is an abundant bird from desertscrub and urban settings well up into the ponderosa pine forest, and Cassin's finch commonly breeds only in the montane mixed-conifer forest openings on the Kaibab Plateau. In winter, Cassin's finches make occasional appearances in many lowland, especially riparian, locations.

Bushtit

Just about the only bird that would be confused with this highly social tiny bird is the verdin, but the two species rarely overlap in habitat and the verdin has a much shorter tail. So if you can just get these actively foraging little fellows to stop a minute.... Travelling about the oak woodland and scrub, at middle-elevations, above the desertscrub but largely below the conifer zone, bushtits are usually seen in flocks of 10 to 20 or so individuals. In the breeding season the groups break up, as some things are indeed better done in pairs, but they reform almost as soon as the young are fledged. While in flocks, bushtits keep up a steady chatter that helps the members locate each other, and which helps birders track the flock.

Cedar Waxwing

The cedar waxwing looks a lot like one of those painted ceramic sculptures offered for sale in magazines. But there is something to be said for a bird that is virtually never seen alone, is reasonably unpredictable, and which seems to favor fermented pyracantha berries on its winter visits to lowland urban areas. Cedar waxwings breed farther north, and their time of arrival in Arizona is as erratic as is their destination and their departure time for the return trip north. But one thing that's certain with this colorful bird is that when you do see one, you will likely see many. Another is that the soft, high-pitched twitterings of the waxwing will be among the first bird sounds you will miss as you begin to appreciate the wonders of presbycussis.

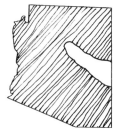

JOHN H. HOFFMAN

Cliff Swallow

The bane of building maintenance crews around Arizona, the cliff swallow is a consummate construction engineer. It simply plasters mud against a concrete or rock face, usually under an overhang, to ensure shade and perhaps some protection from above, until it has a nice single unit house in which to rear its young. Cliff swallow colonies may result in hundreds of nests, and therein lies the problem. Not everyone is enamored with the bird, and even fewer care for its disintegrating mud housing units or its droppings. Fortunately there are thousands of bridge abutments and cliff faces for colonies to use. Rumor has it that when a colony exists over a deep hole in a warm water river, the catfishing there can be excellent. Young swallows do not swim well or for very long.

KEVIN ELLIS

JOHN H. HOFFMAN

Curve-billed Thrasher

Of the six thrashers that occur in Arizona, the curve-billed is by far the best known, by both layman and scientist. It is most common in the desertscrub, especially where chollas abound, but it also resides in brush thickets along lower elevation riparian corridors and in urban settings. Its call is very familiar, a very loud *whit-wheet*, the two notes given very fast and the sequence often being repeated several times. Like other thrashers, the curve-billed never gets far off the ground in flight, and it runs from place to place as often as it flies. Curve-bills may start courtship as early as December, and often begin nesting in January, weather permitting. The nest is a bulky loose stick bowl, with a grass (and sometimes horsehair) lining, and is often built in the arms of a chain cholla.

JOHN H. HOFFMAN

Eastern Bluebird

Thanks to scouts throughout the country, the eastern bluebird enjoys a degree of fame that few species ever attain. The campaign to save the bluebird has been with us for nearly 40 years now, and suffice to say that in its limited range in Arizona, being confined to the southcentral part of the state, the eastern species is alive and well. It is not abundant, though, and it is found in only a relatively few wooded canyons at middle elevations. There, among the evergreen oaks and pines, it finds an abundance of cavities in which to nest, and no need for the nest box programs that have been its salvation in the east.

Mexican Jay

Another victim of changes in naming conventions in the bird world, the once-Mexican, once-Arizona, and once-gray-breasted jay is now again the Mexican jay! The beast itself is still the same highly social, communally breeding bird, with young of previous years helping the parents rear the new crop of youngsters. The Mexican jay is most at home in the evergreen oaks and pine-oak belt of southeastern and central Arizona. It is an Upper Sonoran Life Zone specialist, and does not seem subject to the wide-ranging travels of some other Arizona jays. But like the others, it is an omnivore (with a penchant for acorns), and may occasionally add the young of other birds to its diet.

Hooded Oriole

The pendulous nest of the hooded oriole is a conspicuous element of nature, especially in late fall when riparian deciduous trees have fulfilled their annual obligation to provide leaf litter for ground-dwelling creatures to rummage in. Exposed by the departed leaves, the persistent nests seem inordinately abundant. The colorful birds that built them just don't seem that numerous, yet they must be. Hooded orioles occur fairly widely in Arizona as breeding birds, and winter irregularly in southcentral Arizona. They most commonly breed in southern Arizona, but of late they have expanded their presence above the Mogollon Rim. They are efficient harvesters of invertebrates, and their slightly decurved bills are well suited to gaining access to the nectars in hummingbird feeders.

Hutton's Vireo

One of five nesting species of vireos in this state, Hutton's is a relatively common summer resident of the middle-elevation evergreen oak belt in central and southern Arizona. It shows a remarkable resemblance to the distinctively wing-flicking ruby-crowned kinglet, but its larger size and heavier bill clearly set it apart as a vireo. And, like all vireos, this species is an effective harvester of a variety of canopy-dwelling invertebrates. Hutton's vireo is also a good species for novice birders to practice their *spishing* skills on, as it responds well even to the crudest, most lip-slobbering efforts at attraction.

JOHN H. HOFFMAN

GREG BEATTY

JOHN H. HOFFMAN

JUDD COONEY

Northern Cardinal

It seems as though this bird should not be in Arizona, but it is. Not satisfied with life in the east, it has encroached on territory occupied by its sibling, the pyrrhuloxia. And thank goodness, because the rich color and loud, liquid song of the cardinal are welcome additions anywhere. So, go big red! Most common as a breeding bird in the moister riparian woodlands and wooded canyons of central and southern Arizona, the cardinal has also reached the Colorado River by way of riparian corridors along the major rivers. Though it possesses a powerful seed-cracking bill, in the breeding season the cardinal is also effective at harvesting protein-rich insects to feed its young.

JOHN H. HOFFMAN

Northern Mockingbird

Among the most assertive of urban birds, the mockingbird keeps people awake at night with its song, or the songs and notes it has borrowed from a variety of other birds. It also drives domestic cats crazy, attacking and scolding them, especially when the bird has a nest nearby. Mockingbirds are also widespread in non-urban areas, but they are nowhere as common as in the well-vegetated city. Wherever they occur, they harvest innumerable insects and other invertebrates. A few minutes spent watching them hunt will be richly rewarded. They stand tall and flash their wings, scaring invertebrates into motion. Selection of the unfittest takes place, and the mocker runs or hops to the next foraging site and hopes the cat doesn't take revenge.

Bullock's Oriole

Progress is not without pain, and so it is in the bird world. Not too many years ago taxonomic investigations brought together the Baltimore oriole of the east and the Bullock's oriole of the west and left us with a single, widely-occurring species, the northern oriole. The zone of hybridization between the two forms was too broad to ignore, but thank goodness professional baseball was not obligated to follow the bird world's decision. Now the names have reverted and Bullock's oriole remains alive and well in Arizona, as a summer resident almost statewide. A few parts of the extreme southern part of the state are left behind for exclusive use by hooded orioles. Winter records of Bullock's orioles in Arizona are few and far between, and all from the southeastern area.

Phainopepla

Perched atop a mesquite or an ironwood tree that is heavy laden with parasitic mistletoe clumps, with a softly, but a touch peevishly, whistled *whurrp,* the glossy-black male phainopepla announces to other members of his species that they must find other berries on which to feed. His territory may well include several trees, depending upon how many mistletoe clumps each bears and on how rich each clump is in berries. Phainopeplas occur throughout Arizona, though in the northern parts of the state and at middle-elevations they are only summer residents. These slightly strange looking but very elegant little birds are the mainland United States' only members of a tropical family of birds, the silky flycatchers.

Pyrrhuloxia

The western and arid-lands analog of the northern cardinal, the pyrrhuloxia is perhaps not quite as colorful as its close relative (that is actually highly debatable) but its song, if a bit thinner, is just as melodious. It tends to occur in the drier brush, thickets and scrub, and is less frequent in riparian canyons and more mesic woodlands. It breeds and winters in southcentral and southeastern Arizona, and has appeared in various seasons elsewhere in the state at lower elevations. In winter, pyrrhuloxias may form flocks, and fall back to desert washes as opposed to remaining in the more open desertscrub. Like cardinals, pyrrhuloxias are well suited to taking a variety of foods, including both animal and plant matter.

JOHN H. HOFFMAN

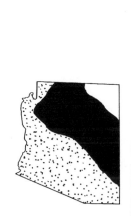

JUDD COONEY

ROBERT CAMPBELL

PAT O'BRIEN

JOHN H. HOFFMAN

RICK BOWERS

Ruby-crowned Kinglet

Ruby-crowned kinglets are as hyperactive as hummingbirds, rapidly moving about in the canopy in search of insect treats, and giving a rather harsh, buzzy call to announce the area is occupied. They never stop flicking their wings, which may indicate the habit has some adaptive significance in flushing prey, or that these birds are simply nervous bundles of energy. In late spring and early summer, males flash the otherwise hidden ruby patch that gives the species its name. The sudden display of color is always a surprise. Fortunately, we even get to see it in the lowland deserts, before wintering kinglets depart for their high-elevation, conifer and spruce forest homes throughout the state.

Spotted Towhee

Unlike their eastern counterparts, western spotted towhees come decorated with bright white spots and splashes. Unfortunately, what we gain in color we lose elsewhere. The towhee's cheery *drink your tea drink your tea* song becomes drier and slightly less musical in the West. Once known as rufous-sided towhees, and perhaps some day they will be again, our western birds sing from canyons, open woodlands, and streamside thickets. Between summer, winter, and migration they can be expected almost anywhere statewide, though primarily at middle elevations. Often they are most conspicuous when noisily scratching their way through deep leaf-litter. Otherwise, except as occasionally around picnic tables, these ground-nesting seedeaters can be a bit elusive. As photogenic as they are, that's a shame.

Rufous-winged Sparrow

Although some grassy desert washes in southcentral Arizona are fairly predictable as to occurrence of this species, by and large as summer rains go, so goes the rufous-winged sparrow. When the rains come, rufous-wings respond with a flurry of nesting behavior. Their bouncing-ball type song begins in earnest, the initial individual notes followed by a rapidly accelerating series of chips. Insects are gathered for the young, and a few weeks later the cycle comes to a close with fledging. The adults occupy the territory through the winter, and are on site and ready to go when summer comes again. Site fidelity has made this species a regular component of ornithology classes at the University of Arizona. The birds respond well to taped calls and demonstrate territorial defense far better than any textbook could ever describe it.

Western Scrub-Jay

A typically gregarious species in the crow family, scrub jays are quite common at middle-elevations throughout Arizona, in open forest and woodland. They are among the most commonly seen birds at many central Arizona campgrounds and recreation sites. They also occur locally in southern Arizona, and in winter may appear almost anywhere, even at lower elevations. The scrub jays of Arizona are not at all endangered; that distinction is left to the isolated population in Florida. Ours are only endangered when a hawk takes advantage of their somewhat loose flocking tendencies, and picks off a straggler or an unwary individual. At 11 to 12 inches in length, a scrub jay makes a healthy meal for a raptor.

RICH BEAUDRY

Summer Tanager

The summer tanager breeds in the oak, and deciduous riparian forests at lower to middle-elevations throughout Arizona. It was also historically common along the major lower-elevation rivers, especially the lower Colorado, but as those riparian gallery forests disappeared, so did the tanager and a host of other species. Fortunately, the summer tanager's loud three-note *pit-a-tuck* (or some reasonable facsimile) and its robin-like song are still among the more common sounds of the Arizona woodlands and forest. Summer tanagers overwinter in Arizona occasionally, usually in lower-elevation riparian forests. Two other reddish tanagers occur in Arizona. The hepatic tanager breeds in the oak-pine and conifer woodlands and higher forests. The scarlet tanager occurs here as a spring or fall vagrant.

ALLAN MORGAN

JOHN H. HOFFMAN

Vermilion Flycatcher

No bird has its name misspelled as consistently as this one (and we hope it's right this time!). The boldly marked male and the equally attractive if a bit more subdued female vermilion make a very handsome couple, and are usually seen together. They forage in openings along streams, rivers, fence rows, irrigated lands and corrals, but are never very far from at least a puddle of surface water. Foraging consists mainly of sallies from a conspicuous perch, into the air or onto the ground. Vermilions are most common in association with mesquites, willows and cottonwoods, in central and southern Arizona. They winter at lower elevations, in areas that are relatively well watered.

Western Bluebird

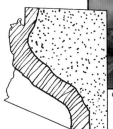

GEORGE ANDREJKO

Like the eastern bluebird, the western is a cavity-nesting bird of forest and woodland. It is much more widely distributed in Arizona than the eastern, though, essentially occurring statewide as a breeding, migrant and wintering bird. More open country and lower elevations are occupied in winter, when westerns form flocks and wander about. Sometimes the aggregations are quite large, but they are prone to be much smaller than the flocks of hundreds that the third Arizona bluebird, the mountain, often forms. Western bluebirds feed on insects throughout the year, but readily take fruits and berries when they are available.

Western Tanager

MIKE PELLEGATTI

The western tanager is more a bird of the open coniferous forests than its cousin, the summer tanager. Both species breed in riparian deciduous forests, too, but the former tends to do so at somewhat higher elevations. The western is most common in Arizona at lower elevations during migration, but few of the birds overwinter here. The song of the western tanager, like that of the summer tanager, is very similar to that of the American robin. And like the summer tanager, the western is an effective insectivore. During migration, though, berries and fruits are also important food sources.

White-breasted Nuthatch

A familiar bird at campsites and recreational developments in the oak-pine and conifer forested mountains almost statewide, the white-breasted is the largest of the three nuthatches in Arizona. It occurs at lower elevations in wooded canyons and riparian forests, and in winter may appear even lower and in more arid habitats. Nuthatches search incessantly for invertebrates and plant materials to eat. The smaller species frequently forage in the outer tree branches, but the white-breasted tends to remain on the trunk and larger limbs, often climbing head first down the tree. Frequently foraging with groups of kinglets, chicadees, and titmice during the non-breeding season, the white-breasted nuthatch nests in cavities and natural crevices in trees.

JOHN H. HOFFMAN

White-throated Sparrow

Every now and again, tucked away among scads of wintering white-crowned, song, and other sparrows, white-throated sparrows make an appearance in Arizona. Most of the records are of single individuals in autumn and early winter, but occasionally larger numbers visit the state, usually in southcentral and southeastern Arizona. White-throats sing the familiar *Old Sam Peabody-Peabody-Peabody* song of eastern United States and Canada forest, farm and garden fame. Various field guides also interpret the song as *sow wheat peverly, peverly, peverly* and *pure sweet Canada Canada Canada.* Regardless of what words are put to the sounds, everyone agrees there are two single notes followed by a three-note phrase repeated three times. In the West, white-throats tend to occupy dense thickets and areas around seeps or streams.

JUDD COONEY

Others . . . .

It seems a little unfair to relegate any birds to the category of "others," even though ornithologists long did this with a family known as the Cotingidae. But, in an overview like this, there is no other option. Some birds just didn't fit the organizational scheme, but we couldn't see how we could exclude them since some photographers had captured them very nicely.

Perhaps foremost among the "other" birds of Arizona are hummingbirds. Our state is truly the hummingbird capital of the United States, with 15 resident or migrant species recorded within its current bounds, actually 16 if you include the Heloise, which is known here from only two specimens collected in 1896. Shoot, some states only have a species or two. In fact, most of the eastern United States only has *one* species, the ruby-throated, which oddly enough has never been documented from Arizona. But, before you bust a button, consider the fact that Mexico and *many* Latin American countries have more than 50 *breeding* species within their bounds.

In addition to hummingbirds, Arizona has a few of their relatives, the swifts. The white-throated swift is probably familiar by sight if not by name to many people. Closely resembling a cigar with wings, it madly paddles its way through the air, chasing flying insects. We also have a few records of chimney swifts (including breeding records), and Vaux's and perhaps black swifts move through in migration. The latter has been reported several times, but our Arizona Bird Committee is a conservative lot and would like to see a bird in the hand, or at least a very good photograph before adding it to our total. Truthfully, the day of the Winchester field glasses has long since passed, and photographic or detailed sight records from recognized experts now suffice as documentation for most occurrences.

Woodpeckers are also among our "other" birds, and we have no shortage in this regard. Twelve species of woodpeckers occur here, and with a stroke of the pen we can expand that by several. The northern flicker is actually a composite of three varieties, the desert-dwelling gilded, the high-elevation red-shafted, and the widely-wintering eastern visitor, the yellow-shafted. If penmanship is not your style, take a more active approach. The sapsucker complex seems to be reorganized every other year, and there must be a new form hiding out there among the red-napes and red- and yellow-breasteds somewhere. Or why not get and beat the bushes today, add a possible pileated from the mountains on the Navajo Nation, and inflate our list by one species?

There are other "other" birds to mention, such as nighthawks and trogons and kingfishers and parrots, but this will have to suffice for now.

Anna's Hummingbird

C. ALLAN MORGAN

Ounce for ounce, Anna's hummingbird is probably as pugnacious a beast as ever wore feathers into battle. Wielding their bills like flashing swords, male Anna's chase each other in a never-ending effort to establish sole control over an energy-rich source of nectar. Place a hummingbird feeder with a 5:1 water:sugar solution in your backyard, and watch the fun begin. For those of us who live at lower elevations, especially in the Phoenix area, watching these hummers battle at the feeder provides constant entertainment from December through May. Anna's is the winter hummingbird in Arizona; although individuals of other species may overwinter here, this one breeds then.

Belted Kingfisher

The loud, dry rattle of a kingfisher is a familiar sound to anglers and hikers who frequent streams and other riparian or wetland settings in Arizona. As long as it has small fish, virtually any water at lower to middle elevations statewide is likely to be visited by these fascinating but rather solitary birds. Few breeding records are known for Arizona, but that is probably more a function of the kingfisher's slightly secretive nesting behavior than of any rarity. Its nest, usually a hole in a creek bank, can be very difficult to find. A related species, the much smaller green kingfisher, also visits Arizona occasionally. Recently, it bred along the San Pedro River, and it should be looked for along streams and small ponds throughout southcentral Arizona.

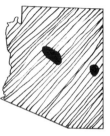

ROBERT CAMPBELL

Blue-throated Hummingbird

One of two large montane hummingbirds in Arizona, at fully 4 to 5 inches long, not including the inch-long bill, the blue-throat is most common in wooded canyons at middle elevations in southeastern Arizona. Its strong, clear whistle (a loud *seeep*), given in flight, is a familar sound to hummingbird watchers in Madera (Santa Rita Mountains), Ramsey (Huachuca Mountains) and Cave Creek (Chiricahua Mountains) canyons. Blue-thoats may reoccupy a nest for several years, but if repairs are necessary they may just add another nest on top of the old one. The penthouse suite may look a bit tipsy when it is perched atop four or five older nests, but it is functional. Sooner or later, though, gravity, or rainfall, will bring it all back to the foundation.

JOHN H. HOFFMAN

C. ALLAN MORGAN

ROBERT CAMPBELL

C. ALLAN MORGAN

Broad-billed Hummingbird

With its dark-tipped, red-based bill, which is slightly decurved, the male broad-billed hummingbird is a welcome sight in the lower to middle elevations of southcentral and southeastern Arizona. Most often seen in desert canyons and riparian woodlands, this species also frequents desert washes. The female's typically drab (for a hummingbird) body plumage lacks the shimmering iridescent blue of the male's, but its bill has at least a dull hint of the reddish base. Broad-bills often play second fiddle to a variety of species when a sugar-water feeder brings them together. Sometimes an auxiliary feeder, off to the side, gives them a chance to quietly replenish their fuel supplies.

Calliope Hummingbird

The calliope is North America's smallest bird, but what a package! The male's striking, purple-red gorget is v-shaped, flaring back impressively on either side of the throat. In Arizona we see this attractive little hummer only in migration, on its way to or from its northwestern United States and Canada breeding grounds. Most of our spotty spring records are from lower elevations in southwestern Arizona, but calliopes also turn up in the fall in middle-elevation canyons, such as the Huachuca Mountains' Ramsey Canyon, and in the northern and eastern parts of the state. There are also reports occasionally from urban backyard feeders in the low desert, so look carefully the next time you have hummers at yours.

Costa's Hummingbird

If you have encountered a hummingbird on a desertscrub-covered southfacing slope or dry desert wash at lower elevations in southern Arizona, it's a good bet that this may have been the bird you saw. On ocotillo covered slopes, Costa's is almost certainly the one. On the small side, even for a hummingbird, the 3-inch long Costa's male is adorned by a brilliant purple (or violet-blue) gorget that sweeps back to either side. The circular flight display of a male with passions, wings, and voice at full throttle is a sight to behold. Males also tend to perch in conspicuous places, affording them ample opportunity to sing their hearts out to anyone who will listen, but without incurring the energy costs of a display flight.

Gila Woodpecker

The southwestern counterpart of the eastern United States' red-bellied woodpecker, the Gila woodpecker is a conspicuous element of Arizona's lower to middle elevation avifauna. It is most abundant in the deserts and riparian woodlands and forests. The typically woodpeckerish undulating flights from perch to perch, in search of elusive grubs, caterpillars and other invertebrates, are announced by raucous *churrr churrr churrr* calls. The noise does not end on arrival, though; sometimes the chorus echoes on endlessly. The Gila is not very selective in its foraging behavior, making good use of trees, cacti, shrubs, and even occasionally working on the ground, in flicker-like fashion. Many of the multi-tenanted nest cavities in saguaros are excavated by this species.

JOHN H. HOFFMAN

Ladder-backed Woodpecker

A much smaller bird than the Gila woodpecker, the ladder-back overlaps broadly with the latter in habitat use. The ladder-back is most abundant in the desertscrub and desert washes, where there are small to medium trees. Mesquites are favorites, for both foraging and nesting. Ladder-backs work their outer branches as well as the main trunks and larger limbs. As pairs of ladder-backs work through an area, they constantly call back and forth to each other. The single note *peeek* and the prolonged rattle *dididididddidididddt* are familiar sounds to urbanites, too. At middle-elevations, where mesquites give way to the oaks and pines, this species gets replaced by Strickland's woodpecker.

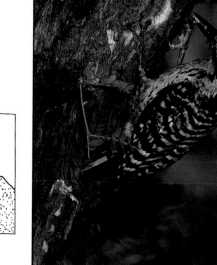

JOHN H. HOFFMAN

Lesser Nighthawk

Goatsucker. Nightjar. Bullbat. A rose by any name, the lesser nighthawk is fun to watch. As light on their wings as hummingbirds, nighthawks pick their food up on the fly. Much lower flying than its close relative, the common nighthawk, the lesser sweeps over the open desertscrub as day breaks or evening settles in, and flying insects spring to life. Given on the wing, the low, soft but rapid trill of this species has an insect-like quality that is very different than the explosive *peernt peernt* of the common nighthawk. Watching foraging nighthawks at baseball stadium lights can be viewed as either a pleasant respite from a boring game, or an intrusion in an exciting pitchers' duel.

C. ALLAN MORGAN

JUDD COONEY

PAT O'BRIEN

PAT O'BRIEN

Lewis's Woodpecker

At 10 inches in length, Lewis's woodpecker is a very large woodpecker for Arizona. Typically inhabiting the pine forests in the eastcentral and northern parts of the state, this species also occasionally makes winter appearances in orchards at lower elevations, as in pecan groves near Tucson. It is most often seen making long sallies out from exposed perches, to take insects on the wing. Its flight is distinctly unwoodpeckerlike, as it is direct and flat and lacks the undulations that characterize the flights of our other woodpeckers. Lewis's woodpecker also stores acorns and nuts in cavities in trees and telephone or fence poles, much like the more famous and colonial acorn woodpecker.

Northern Flicker

There are three varieties of flickers in Arizona, and at one point they were considered three species. But interbreeding was documented, and the lifelists of countless birders were reduced by two. Now it's back up a notch, to the gilded and the northern flickers. The northern flicker (including both red-shafted and yellow-shafted forms) occurs statewide, and occupies a broad variety of habitats. The gilded flicker tends to occupy lower elevation habitats, including desert scrub and riparian woodlands and forests. In its red-shafted form, it tends to inhabit middle to higher elevation forests and woodlands. The yellow-shafted form is a sparse transient and winter visitor most anywhere.

Thick-billed Parrot

Foraging thick-bills once dangled from cone-laden conifers in middle to upper elevation forests throughout the southwestern United States and Mexico. Largely extirpated from the northerly parts of their historical range at the turn of the century, thick-bills had not been documented as occurring in the United States since 1938. In 1986, the Department, in cooperation with several agencies and Wildlife Preservation Trust, International, began a reestablishment program for this species in southeastern Arizona. The effort has been marked by successes and setbacks, and it is still too early to tell whether reestablishment can be achieved, but hope springs eternal in conservationists everywhere.

KEVIN ELLIS

Birding Basics

If you wish to begin birdwatching now, *today*, how should you begin? Well, there is no single right or wrong way, but there is some advice that will help make the experience enjoyable and perhaps promote a bit of longevity. Contrary to many recreational pursuits, it is not necessary to spend a fortune to begin enjoying birdwatching, although there is plenty of time to do that after you are hooked.

Books are essential to birdwatching, and the Arizona beginner should buy at least two. One should be either the National Geographic Society's *Field Guide to the Birds of North America* (1987, second edition), Peterson's *A Field Guide to Western Birds* (1990, third edition), or Robbins, Bruun, Zim and Singer's *Birds of North America: A Guide to Field Identification* (1983, revised edition). The choice is actually often irrelevant, because once smitten you will buy the other two. And once seriously committed, or ready to be committed, you will feel absolutely compelled to add *The Audubon Society Master Guide to Birding* (1983, Parts 1, 2 and 3), edited by J. Farrand. Regardless of how many field guides are purchased, you must buy Davis and Russell's *Finding Birds in Southeastern Arizona* (1995) or Lane's *A Birder's Guide to Southeastern Arizona* (1995, revised by R.C. Taylor). These two books will help you find some of the best areas in which to find the birds the other books will help identify. None of the essential books will require you to spend more than $20, but the master guide series will take about twice that much.

Oddly enough, special optical equipment is not essential to this activity.
. . . the intensity of your participation will dictate the amount of your investment.

Oddly enough, special optical equipment is not essential to this activity. Unaided but careful observation at a backyard feeder, from an inconspicuous vantage point, can reveal all the fine detail of most any avian visitor. But, if you wish to examine individual feathers as well as overall plumage, or see distant or flying birds well, binoculars and spotting scopes will be crucial to your success. Even then, the intensity of your participation will dictate the amount of your investment.

For casual birdwatching, a few minutes or a few hours here and there, $60 to $75 will buy an adequate pair of binoculars. If you wish to spend several hours each day or on any one day using field glasses and spotting scopes, without suffering an eyestrain headache the likes of which druggists have never imagined even in their wildest nightmares, spend a little more (or a whole lot more), say about $200 to $1500. That price range will unveil glass so clear you will think it is not even there, armor coating to keep out the incessant drizzle that follows birdwatchers, and zoom lenses that let you focus at most any magnification from 7x to 10x (binoculars) or 15x to 60x (scopes). Add a $25 tripod and perhaps a window-mount for the spotting scope and you are almost in business.

All you need now is field clothes and note keeping materials. The clothing is easy. Just choose anything that you won't mind getting rain and mud soaked, torn by barbed wire, cactus spines or thorns, and drab enough to be inconspicuous but with enough color to separate you from a deer or a javelina during seasons when that sort of recognition is important. Unless you are headed for social birding circles, even discarded housepainting clothing can be used. Just make sure it's cut loose enough to allow freedom of movement, but not so loose that you will high center when crossing a fence. And the more pockets the better, for books, notepads, snacks, bandannas (to clean your glasses and mop your brow) and a million other little things the well-equipped birder accumulates but rarely uses.

As for notekeeping, you can buy all kinds of packaged journals and note-books for $10 to $40, and use them a time or two before you discard them because they do not meet your needs. Or you can buy a school kid's 5 1/2 x 8 1/2 three-ring notebook with lined paper, add copies of whatever 10¢ bird checklists exist for your target area, a #2 1/2 pencil or a pen with waterproof ink. Armed with this equipment, which is much the same as the schedule-keeping battle gear of every brave yuppie entrepreneur, you can make notes for every birdwatching bout and have a year-end chronology that will help generate those most important of all documents: lists of all the birds you saw in the last calendar year and all the birds you have seen in your life. As you become firmly gripped by the obsession, you can add other lists, too: country lists, state lists, day lists, yard lists, back yard lists, front yard lists, county lists, rainy-day in Georgia lists.... The list of lists is endless.

Finally, just as birds of a feather flock together, so do birdwatchers. The National Audubon Society has seven chapters in Arizona: Phoenix, Prescott, Sedona, Sierra Vista, Tucson, the White Mountains, and Yuma. Each of them holds a monthly meeting from September through May, and most of them take the summer off (to go birding!). Chapter membership is generally about $5, and membership in the national organization runs about $30 per year. Most chapters sponsor field trips (car-pooling is de rigueur, so a vehicle is not even essential), some of which are devoted entirely to people who wish to learn how to birdwatch. They also publish monthly newsletters that are filled with useful information on recent "good" birds (unusual sightings, etc.) and all kinds of environmental news. And National Audubon's glossy bimonthly magazine is world famous for its content and appearance.

Regular membership meetings and field trips are not the only organized birding events to be enjoyed in Arizona, or elsewhere for that matter. The social and scientific highlight of the birdwatching year is the Christmas Bird Count, in which a few to several dozen participants spend an entire day covering a specific area in an effort to count every bird within it. Nationwide, more than 40,000 birders are involved in these counts each year, and thank goodness they are! Coupled with Breeding Bird Surveys and Breeding Bird Censuses in late spring and early summer, Christmas counts give management agencies a wealth of data on which to base evaluations of population trends and management concerns. And it all stems from the efforts of novice to highly-skilled volunteers who may have nothing in common but an interest in birds, and nature.

In 1500 words it is simply not possible to cover even all the basics that will help you get started birdwatching. But hopefully we have given you enough to whet your appetite. If you are still a bit hesitant, try a trip to your local public library. Peruse some of the books mentioned above, or Buff's *The Birder's Catalogue* (1989). The latter is a compendium of information on how to start birdwatching, where to do it, what books and records to use, bird art appreciation and collecting, and, finally, how to turn birdwatching into an obsession: birding. If you start the book, and practice what you read as you read it, reading the last chapter will be entirely unnecessary. You will already be among the devoted enthusiasts of what may well be the largest participatory outdoor recreational activity of the decade.

There is also a final benefit to be gained from birdwatching. When you inspire others to take up the sport, you absolutely assure yourself that you will never again have to ponder the age old question: What can I give this person for this special occasion? A birdwatcher can never have enough books, t-shirts, hats, field equipment, bumper stickers and the like. And if that is not enough, just give them a plane ticket to anywhere in the world. They are certain to see new and exciting birds there, perhaps enough so that they will not notice until a wee bit too late that the ticket you gave them only covers one way. Then you won't need to listen to them any more, as they describe the pleasures of birdwatching. And in your newly found quiet, you may decide to explore the subject yourself.

Hummingbirds
of Arizona

By **Terry B. Johnson**
Nongame Branch Chief

Rufous Hummingbird
Photo by Rick & Nora Bowers

Birds are beautiful, and none dazzle the eye more than hummingbirds. Zipping from flower to flower, they are sights to behold. And most of us would, if they'd stop long enough for our eyes to focus. Ironically, when they do give us a good look, what catches our eye is an illusion. For the flaming orange-red throat of a rufous hummingbird is not orange-red at all, just as the aptly named blue-throated hummingbird is absent any blue. But more about that later. Hummingbirds are masters of deception when it comes to color as well as fascinating in many other ways. In this special Arizona Wildlife Views pull-out section, in a reasonably light-hearted fashion, we'll show and tell you why.

By Terry B. Johnson
Nongame Branch Chief

THE NUMBERS GAME

Arizona's list of hummers stands at 17 species. The only state with more is Texas. California and New Mexico have just a few less than we do, but the rest of the country is way behind. Many eastern states are home to just one breeding species: the ubiquitous ruby-throat.

Arizona is famed for its hummers, and for being home to the "Hummingbird Capital of America" (various places here lay claim to that title). Alas, the boast is just another deception, although this one can't be laid at the feet of the hummingbirds. When it comes to hummers, the true capital must be well south of us.

Mexico has 51 species and Ecuador has more than 150! In fact, many South and Central American countries have at least twice as many species as all of North America, north of Mexico. So, chirp up the next time someone boasts about Arizona's 17 species, or the 24 known from the United States and Canada.

WHY NOT MORE?

Hummingbirds are uniquely Western Hemisphere treasures. Sunbirds, which are the same as hummers in form and function, are their Old World counterparts. The number of species exceeds 340 rangewide, peaking in South America and dropping off toward the north. The drop off is because basic natural laws of anatomy and physiology dictate that a "warm-blooded" animal as small as a hummingbird burns energy at a rate about which human weight watchers can only fantasize. Energy is hard to come by in cold country, and frozen nectar is tough to drink.

From a human perspective, eating like a hummingbird would be a problem, not a solution. It takes lots of nectar and invertebrates to fuel those engines. A hummer consumes about 50 percent of its body weight in sugar each day, but may drink several times its body weight in fluids, which shows that burning energy like a hummer, not eating like a one, would be best for weight challenged folks. To do

that, all you'd have to do is fly. Forward, backward, and upside down, all day long. Oh, and while you eat, don't forget to hover, the most energy-expensive flight of all.

The bottom line: the United States and Canada are nice summer homes for hummers, but come fall and cold weather, these tiny beasts find themselves a warmer clime, where insects and flower nectar abound.

THE HIGH COST OF TRAVEL

Hummers don't fly by jet, but that doesn't stop them from making long seasonal journeys. The western species generally migrate along corridors in or near the Rocky Mountains of Canada, the United States, and Mexico. The one-way trip for a rufous far exceeds 1,000 miles. Weather and food abundance may dictate the pace at which they move. They can replenish supplies at the next scheduled stop, or a few miles down the road.

But what about those eastern ruby-throats? Twice each year they encounter an obstacle known as the Gulf of Mexico. It's a 500-mile flight, one way, with few opportunities for "Gee, I'm tired so I'd better find a motel" stopovers. How can a bird so small pack enough energy for such a trip? The over-simplified answer is plain old fat. This energy-rich substance is laid down when the living is easy. A gram or so of fat and a hummer is ready to go 'round the world in 80 days. Or so it seems. All the bird has to do is drain the nectar from a thousand or so flowers to meet its basic needs, and more to lay down that gram of fat.

FORM AND FUNCTION

Hummingbirds are small. Everyone knows that. But how small are they, and why aren't they smaller? Or bigger? Again, the laws of anatomy and physiology prevail. Most hummers weigh 4 to 5 grams, which is not quite 0.2 ounces, about the same as a nickel. They range from 2 grams (the bee hummingbird, of Cuba) to 22 grams (the giant hummingbird, of South America).

Weight-wise, it takes about 50,000 hummingbirds to equal an ostrich.

Having agreed that hummingbirds are small and that if they were any larger they would be other birds, since space is short we can move on to other facts. A hummingbird is tied for the world's smallest bird or mammal: at 2 grams, the bee hummingbird is equaled in stature only by the pygmy shrew (southern Europe and North Africa), and Kitti's hog-nosed bat (Thailand).

In comparison to body size, hummingbirds have the largest hearts of any bird and the fastest heartbeat, peaking at about 1,200 per minute. Think about that heartbeat the next time yours begins to race, at 125 to 175. Hummer feathers are more densely packed than those of most any other bird. Their breast muscles, which are about 25 percent of their body weight, and their brains are proportionately bigger than those of any other feathered creature. The whole package operates at fever pitch, about 104 degrees.

THE REST OF THE STORY

About that color thing. Basically, hummers are drab. Their feathers, at least in terms of pigments, are absent most of those colors we see. But not to worry. Hummers just substitute a little feather structure for pigment and we humans are no less pleased; simple minds, simple pleasures. Their tiny feathers are structured so they reflect (refract) sunlight differentially and generate those flashy iridescent colors. In truth, that's not so unusual in the bird world. Hummers have just made it an art form.

Most male hummingbirds have at least a patch of iridescence. Often the most spectacular color is on the throat, in which case the emerald green, ruby red, baby blue, or passionate purple patch is known as a gorget. Some hummers have equally brilliant crowns. Even the typically more drab females sometimes have a bit of brilliance here or there.

Regardless, it's all form, not substance (pigment). Microscopic barbules that hook the feathers together reflect light and make us see color where pigment is not. The only pigments here are melanins that appear blackish or rufous to us. The melanin granules are important, however, in helping bend light that falls on the feathers in such a way that we see colors. It's complex, and perhaps more indirect than simple pigmentation, but what a spectacular result. And the final effect changes with every slight adjustment in our angle of sight. Want a

different shade of red, or a greenish tinge? Move your head a tiny bit. Or wait a second for the hummer to move.

BEHAVIOR

Hummingbird behavior fascinates as much as hummingbird colors. The courtship rituals of these birds are often complex, with the male performing an elaborate flight that brings the female's heart to that 1,200 beats per minute peak. Some even add a weak but energetic song to their effort to win a heart. If the display is successful, male and female come together for

just long enough to ensure that the next generation will begin. Once mating is over, he's out-of-sight and she's out-of-mind. He returns to his old habits and another conquest, and she begins the rigors of nest building, egg laying, and incubation. Don't tell me that females don't hold the world together. After 14 to 21 days of incubation (the duration is species specific), the usual two eggs produce naked, helpless young which the female feeds for 2 1/2 to 5 weeks until they reach fledging age. Even after fledging, the youngsters may continue to receive care from the female.

Another behavioral note relates back to metabolism. Although hummingbirds are high energy beasts, they can cool the fires and temporarily reduce the metabolic cost of life. This brings us to torpor, and rest. Hummers are the only birds that regularly enter a state of torpor each night. Their body temperature drops, in some cases more than 50 degrees. While torpid, their heartbeat slows down, to as low as 50 or 100 beats per minute. In this state, they consume far less energy, eliminating the

A calliope hummingbird
Photo by
Paul & Shirley Berquist

Weight-wise, it takes about 50,000 hummingbirds to equal an ostrich.

THERE'S ALWAYS MORE TO LEARN
A few words about further information. Don't forget the old standards: field guides to birds and nests. Unfortunately, they are too numerous to list here, but every birdwatcher's library should include them. Some good, in-print, hummingbird references include

Engel-Wilson, C. 1992. Landscaping for desert wildlife. Arizona Game and Fish Department, Phoenix. Don't landscape in Phoenix or Tucson without it!

Grant, K.A. and V. Grant. 1968. Hummingbirds and their flowers. Columbia University Press, New York.

Lazaroff, D.W. 1995. The secret lives of hummingbirds. Arizona-Sonora Desert Museum Press, Tucson.

Stokes, D. and L. Stokes. 1989. The hummingbird book: the complete guide to attracting, identifying, and enjoying hummingbirds. Little, Brown and Company; Boston, Toronto, and London. Packed with good information, and very well illustrated.

Toops, C.M. 1992. Hummingbirds: jewels in flight. Voyageur Press, Inc., Minnesota. Wow! A book both gorgeous and incredibly fun to read. The Arizona stories are great.

need for midnight snacks. Tropical species tend to have milder body temperature adjustments, as might be expected in their warmer climes.

Broad-billed hummingbird Photo by G.C. Kelley

ATTRACTING AND FEEDING HUMMINGBIRDS ——
Attracting hummingbirds is easy almost anywhere in Arizona. Just landscape with brightly flowering shrubs, trees, and wildflowers. Red, orange, and pink are the favorite flower colors, but yellow also draws its share of hummers. Among the many southwestern plants that hummers love are penstemon, paintbrush, ocotillo, honeysuckle, chuparosa, coral bean, gilia, cardinal flower, sage, columbine, and bouvardia. Aside from bright colors, these tubular flowers all have one thing in common: their nectar is 20 to 30 percent sucrose. Plants such as ocotillo and desert willow offer twice the benefits, in that they also provide nest sites for hummers.

A little creative landscaping with low-maintenance plants is all you need, but "nectar" feeders will add to your fun by attracting even more hummers, and other native birds such as orioles, verdins, and house finches. The best feeders are easy to clean and hard to spill, and discourage bees and wasps. But remember, a feeder that bees and wasps can't use will probably not be accessible to orioles and house finches, either. Use several kinds, and enjoy watching these other birds, too

Place your feeder out of direct sunlight and fairly close to shrubs or trees. Then hummers can perch in the shade and watch "their" feeders, and protect them from intruders. These little warriors will make lightning-like attacks on their competitors, and the fight-chases are fun to watch.

The feeder's contents should always be four cups of water to one cup of cane or table sugar (it's sucrose, just like flowers produce). Stronger solutions may harm the birds. Never use sugar substitutes, and honey spoils quickly and grows fungus that may be lethal to hummers. There's no need to use dye in the solution. Red plastic, paint, or tape on the feeder is just as effective in attracting the bird's attention. To prepare the solution—boil water, add sugar, and let the mix cool. Fill the feeder with as much solution as will be used in a day or two. This is a bit more work, but assures the hummers a fresh food supply daily. Extra mix can be refrigerated for a week or two, while it is used for refills.

Feeders should always be kept at least partially filled and very clean, or else they should be taken down. Always take them down when they will not be attended daily. Clean them at least every five to seven days (more often in warm weather), using baby-bottle brushes or pipe cleaners and hot water. A slurry of equal parts table salt and water works well. A small dose of vinegar helps remove mold, but rinse the feeder very well afterward! Never use detergent or soap.

Landscaping with desert plants and avoiding use of insecticides will help give hummers in your area a balanced diet. Add a feeder or two and you can enjoy countless hours of fast-action birdwatching, year-round. Don't worry about taking your feeder down in winter. Just keep it filled, and clean.

Ants and bees are the bane of picnics and hummingbird feeders. If your feeder lacks "ant moats," to keep ants away spread liberal amounts of petroleum jelly or mineral oil on the wire from which your feeder hangs. Double-sided sticky tape wrapped around the wire also works well. As for bees, spread a little petroleum jelly around the feeder openings. The jelly's odor won't bother the hummers, since like most birds they have a very poorly developed sense of smell. For a gentler, kinder approach: accept the ants and bees as a natural consequence of feeding hummers, and plant a garden with non-hummingbird flowers to distract the bees.

ACKNOWLEDGMENTS ————————————
Many thanks to Troy Corman, Ron Engel-Wilson, Tracy McCarthey, Susan Sferra, Sheri Williamson, and Tom Wood for constructive comments on this article. The remaining errors are mine. And special thanks to Bill Calder and Steve and Ruth Russell, whose hummingbird studies have long been an inspiration.

Anna's Hummingbird
(Calypte anna)

Photo by
Paul & Shirley Berquist

The flaming crimson to rose gorget and crown of the male are exactly what comes to mind when most people think of hummingbirds: a brilliant splash of color on a fast moving, tiny bird.

At 4 inches and 4+ grams, Anna's is a mid-sized Arizona hummingbird. Gram for gram, though, it's as pugnacious a beast as ever wore feathers into battle. Wielding its bill like a flashing sword, Anna's fearlessly chases intruders in a never-ending quest for sole control over a nectar source. For those of us who live at lower elevations in Arizona, Anna's provides almost year-round entertainment.

By any measure, Anna's is spectacular. The flaming crimson to rose gorget and crown of the male are exactly what comes to mind when most people think of hummingbirds: a brilliant splash of color on a fast moving, tiny bird. Even the female has a sprinkling of red in her otherwise grayish throat. Both sexes are gray below, with a green back. The male tops his gaudy dress by giving a display song while perched or in flight. Well, it's a song by hummingbird standards: anything even slightly melodious. In reality, the song is a jumbled series of squeaky, even raspy, phrases. To some people it sounds like nine-inch nails on chalkboard. Noises may help ward off other hummers. Sheri Williamson and Tom Wood, while managers at Arizona's Ramsey Canyon Preserve, said "Our observations suggest the singing, screeching, and tail fanning displays all help this species limit actual physical combat (unlike rufous, which seem to hit first and ask questions later)."

Anna's breeds along the West Coast from southwestern British Columbia to Baja California. Wanderers have been noted as far north as southeastern Alaska. The southern end of the range extends into southeastern Arizona from California. Nevada records are as scarce as rich old gamblers. Anna's spills over into northwestern Sonora, Mexico, too.

Like those on some of the Channel Islands and the adjacent California coast, some Arizona populations are resident, especially in Phoenix and Tucson. Other areas are occupied seasonally. Active nests have been found in our desert lowlands as early as mid-November, but are more common in late winter and early spring. Cemeteries, backyards, and other well-watered habitats are favored nest sites in urban settings. The water is probably less important to the hummers than the insects found around such habitats. Cottonwood-willow riparian habitats are favored in non-urban desert lowlands. With the onset of hot weather, Anna's vacate the southern deserts and show up at middle elevations (usually below about 6,000 feet) in south-central Arizona.

Much of what is known about hummingbird behavior has been learned from studies of this species. Scientists such as Gary Stiles in southern California have generated superb information about time-energy budgets, territoriality, breeding behavior, and physiology (including torpidity). Many of these studies have been of free-ranging birds, so they are all the more impressive.

BERYLLINE HUMMINGBIRD

(Amazilia beryllina)

Photo by
Rick & Nora Bowers

They are best known from wooded canyons in the southeastern part of the state, in the Chiricahuas, Huachucas, and Santa Ritas. Nesting has been confirmed in Arizona a few times since 1976, but don't count on seeing this species each year. To do that, you must travel south. This hummer frequents the montane forests, moist canyons, and foothills of Mexico's Sierra Madre and on south into Central America (Guatemala, El Salvador, and Honduras).

In Arizona, beryllines have been seen most often in mid-elevation canyons (ca. 5,000 feet), especially those with flowering thistles. There are no winter records for the United States. The first nest discovered here (in 1976) was in oak woodland at the American Museum of Natural History's Southwestern Research Station, in the Chiricahuas. Beryllines in the Huachucas have tended toward canyon bottom riparian habitats. They construct a typical hummer nest: twigs and similar materials held together and suspended by spiderwebs, and adorned by lichens. At the first nest recorded in Arizona, I watched the female pull cotton from a volleyball net to embellish the bowl that would soon hold her eggs. Fortunately, no game was underway!

At least one author has described the berylline's singing voice as "better than the average hummingbird." I've heard beryllines sing a few times, and I would describe their efforts as: energetic, and not without result. But why argue? Rating singing ability is such a personal exercise.

The berylline and its cousins, the violet-crown and cinnamon (which also occur in Arizona), belong to a genus whose members are both ubiquitous and abundant in Central and South America. The genus *Amazilia* includes more than 30 species. Our three species, while gorgeous in their own right, are a mere hint of what awaits a visit to the ecological metropolis of the genus: the Latin American lowlands and coffee zone.

M id-size by Arizona standards, the berylline hummingbird attains a body length of about 4.25 inches and a weight of 4.25 to 5.75 grams. The male has a glittering green chest, and a gray to brown abdomen. Above, it is equally green on the crown and upper back, with a chestnut lower back that blends with a purple-chestnut rump. The central tail feathers are purple, and the outer ones are rufous with purple tips. The wings have a beautiful rufous patch not found on any other American hummer. The upper bill is black, the lower one reddish. The female is also beautiful, with colors similar to those of the male, though somewhat duller, with more gray. Young beryllines have completely black bills.

Unfortunately, beryllines are neither common nor regular in occurrence in Arizona.

BLACK-CHINNED HUMMINGBIRD

The black-chin is 3.5 inches long and weighs 3 to 3.5 grams, well within the mid-range for Arizona hummingbirds. The western counterpart of the ruby-throat, it is widespread and locally abundant. Males have unremarkable dark metallic green upperparts, but their black chin is bordered below by an iridescent purple-violet band layered above a pale-white chest. The total effect is remarkable in strong light. The rest of the male's underparts are greenish-gray. The female is merely green above and whitish below, with an immaculate to slightly stained throat and a tinge of buff on the flanks.

Where both occur, female black-chinned hummers cannot safely be distinguished from female ruby-throated hummers in the field. Fortunately, ruby-throats don't occur in Arizona, but that still leaves us to distinguish possible female black-chins from possible female Anna's, or Costa's, or even broad-tails. For the beginner, or someone who sees these birds only rarely, that isn't easy, despite what the field guides say. So be prepared, expect disappointment, and try again. Look closely at the outer tail feathers, and study the field guides. You can do it! Hints: the black-chin has a distinctive call and proportionately long and slightly drooping bill.

The breeding range of this species extends from British Columbia and Montana south through the Rockies and California, Arizona, New Mexico, and southwestern Texas into northern Mexico. The winter range is in Mexico, as far south as Michoacan. Much of southern Arizona is occupied by black-chins from mid-March through October. They breed in riparian and other mesic conditions (wooded springs and seeps) at mid-elevations, and are frequently encountered in canyons. They also breed in urban residential areas, and in some pinyon-juniper habitats. In insect rich settings, female black-chins have been known to fledge young twice in a single breeding season.

One of my favorite Arizona memories is of a black-chin nest at Fort Bowie National Historic Site, in the Chiricahua Mountains. In the middle of a hot July day in 1976, I found a nest at Apache Spring. The nest, a typical twig-and-spiderweb-covered-by-lichen affair, was in a small shrub, well shaded by lush trees. The ambient temperature there seemed 50 degrees cooler than out where the whiptail lizards crawled. Over the next three hours, I watched the female make dozens of food-bearing trips to the nest, and stuff the insects she was catching down the gullets of her two youngsters. All the while, 10 feet away from me and a few feet below the nest, a 3.5-foot black-tailed rattlesnake lay coiled, waiting for a meal that never came.

(Archilochus alexandri)

Male black-chinned photo by G.C. Kelley

Female with young photo by Paul A. Berquist

Males have unremarkable dark metallic green upperparts, but their black chin is bordered below by an iridescent purple-violet band layered above a pale-white chest.

BLUE-THROATED HUMMINGBIRD

(Lampornis clemenciae)

Photo by
G.C. Kelley

Sometimes blue-throats hold their large wings still while flying, as if to rest them, and glide like a swift.

The 5.25-inch long, 7- to 8.5-gram blue-throat is Arizona's largest hummer. It beats out the magnificent by a quarter inch or so. The male blue-throat's powder blue gorget, lacking in the female, is distinctive but can be difficult to see. Both sexes have a bold white eye stripe, a fainter white whisker stripe (shorter in the female), gray-brown crown and upperparts, dark gray underparts, and very conspicuous broad white tips on the three outer tail feathers.

Males have a distinctive territorial call, a loud, high *seeep*, or *seeek*, often described as a clear, piercing whistle. During the extended chases in which these birds engage, the whistles are often easier to follow through the woods than the birds giving them. The blue-throat's flight is fast and loud, but seems labored. Sometimes blue-throats hold their large wings still while flying, as if to rest them, and glide like a swift.

Blue-throats range from southern Arizona and New Mexico and southwestern Texas to southern Mexico. They are occasionally noted in Colorado, Utah, California, and Nevada. In Arizona, their distribution is centered in Cochise, Pima, and Santa Cruz counties, but reaches Oak Creek Canyon and other Mogollon Rim settings such as Christopher Creek. Spring arrival begins by late March; fall departure occurs by October. Wintering blue-throats have been reported from protected canyons in Arizona's southeastern mountains. Insects that emerge during warm spells, in what passes for winter down there, are an important food source for wintering birds.

In southeastern Arizona, the blue-throat is most common in wooded canyons at 5,000 or more feet. Cave Creek (Chiricahua Mountains), Madera (Santa Rita Mountains), and Ramsey (Huachuca Mountains) canyons are among its favorite haunts. Many of these areas support free-flowing perennial streams. A perch along a stream offers good opportunities for announcing possession of a territory and all that goes with it.

The nest is the usual blend of twigs and other plant materials bound together by spiderwebs. Unique among our hummers, the blue-throat decorates its nest with living green mosses plucked from streamside rocks. The nest is invariably built under something, usually near running water. Some are attached to tree limbs, others are under bridges or the eaves of streamside houses or carports. Females may reoccupy nests for several years, sometimes building a new nest atop an old one until the penthouse suite is four or five stories up. Sooner or later, gravity and rain bring the leaning tower down. Hopefully not during the 17- to 18-day incubation period for the two white eggs, or during the 24- to 29-day nestling period. Triple-clutching (three sets of eggs in a single breeding season) has been noted in this species.

BROAD-BILLED HUMMINGBIRD

(Cynanthus latirostris)

Photo by
G.C. Kelley

The broad-bill is about 4 inches long and weighs 3.5 to 3.75 grams. The male has a glittering blue-green throat, blue-spackled green breast, dark green upperparts, and forked blue-black (indigo) tail. The overall appearance is so dark that, when not catching the sun properly, broad-bills appear black. In full sun, they are such bright blue they seem to glow. The female is also greenish above, but its underparts are pearly gray or off-white, and conspicuously unmarked. Her outer tail feathers are white tipped. In both sexes the bill is red with a black or dusky tip, though the female's is sometimes duller.

Broad-bills breed from southern Arizona, New Mexico, and west Texas into central Mexico. In winter, most withdraw from the northern part of the range. A few winter in Tucson. In all seasons they inhabit desert canyons, riparian settings, and adjacent arid slopes. In Arizona, they are most frequent in the southeast, below 5,000 feet. Among the more reliable places are Patagonia (Sonoita Creek) and especially Madera Canyon (Santa Rita Mountains). Broad-bills are regular at the well-stocked feeders in The Nature Conservancy's Mile Hi Preserve in Ramsey Canyon, but are rare in comparison to the abundant Anna's, black-chins, and various other hummers.

Arriving on its Arizona breeding grounds in March to early April, the broad-bill announces its presence with gusto. The chattery *jiit*, or *jedit*, is given by both sexes. Most field guides compare the male's soft, ventriloqual, and not at all musical song to that of a ruby-crowned kinglet. I prefer ornithologist Bill Baltosser's comparison: a broad-bill's song is like the sound made by small steel balls rattling in one's hand.

At Ramsey Canyon, Mile Hi managers Sheri Williamson and Tom Wood noted a peculiar behavior unique to the broad-bill. After touching down on a perch, it shivers its wings and tail. The movement is distinctly different from the tail pumping of other species, such as the black-chin and Costa's.

The broad-bill's nest is somewhat rougher and more loosely constructed than those of other hummingbirds with which it sometimes occurs (e.g. Costa's, black-chin). It is usually affixed to a small branch in a shrub or low tree, and decorated with brown bark, dried leaves, and bits of grass, rather than the lichens used by many other hummers. Regardless, it still has room for the usual complement of two eggs, and the spiderweb that binds it all together stretches to accommodate the nestlings as they grow. By late August or early September, the young have fledged and most broad-bills are soon back in Mexico.

CALLIOPE HUMMINGBIRD
(Stellula calliope)

BROAD-TAILED HUMMINGBIRD
(Selasphorus platycercus)

Broad-tailed photo by
Robert A. Sutton

Calliope photo by
Rick & Nora Bowers

The broad-tail is 4 inches long and weighs 3 to 4 grams. Both sexes are metallic iridescent green above. The male's gorget is brilliant rose pink. His other underparts are mostly white, with green flanks and cinnamon green undertail coverts. His unforked tail has green central feathers; the others are bluish black with inconspicuous rufous outer edges. The female's throat is off-white with red spackles. Her flanks are buffy, her tail feathers rufous at the base (the outer ones are broadly tipped white). In both sexes the bill is black.

Broad-tails breed in the mountains from southeastern Oregon, Idaho, and Wyoming through southern Arizona, New Mexico, and west Texas to Guatemala. They begin arriving in Arizona in early March and become relatively abundant by mid-April. By May, those bound for farther north have moved through. Northern breeders return in August and September on the way back to Mexico to winter.

Male broad-tails are easily recognized. Just use your ears. In flight, the male's flight feathers produce a whistling sound like a cricket chirp, or the *zinnngggg* made by running a finger down the teeth of a comb. It can be heard up to 100 yards away, but as the wing feathers wear down, the whistle fades. It returns in full vigor with the next molt.

At 2.8 to 3.5 inches and 2 to 3 grams, the calliope is America's smallest breeding bird. The male's long metallic rose-purple gorget feathers are elongated toward the sides and extend across an otherwise white throat. His crown and back are iridescent green, with a bluish tinge. His underparts are whitish, suffused with green on the abdomen and buff on the flanks. The female is also metallic green above, but lacks a gorget and has more buff or cinnamon on its chest, abdomen, and flanks. In both sexes the bill is short and black, the tail is stubby and unforked.

Calliopes breed from southwestern Canada through Washington and Idaho into California and even locally in Baja California. They frequent streams in mountain meadows and canyons, occurring most commonly at 4,000 to 8,000 feet. They winter in Mexico. Arizona provides habitat during spring and (especially) fall migration.

The calliope calls with a high-pitched *tsew*. Both call and bird are easily lost in the crowd when thundering herds of more common hummers are present. But when a calliope does catch someone's eye or ear, the alert sounds and all available binoculars focus in so observers can check the little prize off their lists. Size and a spectacular gorget are not the only conspicuous things about the calliope. Unlike many hummers, this one doesn't pump its tail while hovering to feed. Its stubby tail remains still, and angled up.

This species is known from Arizona on the basis of two female specimens. They were reported from Ramsey Canyon (Huachuca Mountains) on July 2, 1896. The identification is correct, but the locality is questionable. No bumblebee hummingbirds have been taken within hundreds of miles of the United States since the Arizona specimens were collected. At 2.25 inches, the bumblebee would be America's smallest bird, if one would only visit us (again?).

BUMBLEBEE HUMMINGBIRD
(Atthis heloisa)

LUCIFER HUMMINGBIRD

(Calothorax lucifer)

Bumblebee photo by
Rick & Nora Bowers

Lucifer photo by
Rick & Nora Bowers

Cinnamon photo by
J. Dunning/VIREO

CINNAMON

(Amazilia rutila)

The 4.25-inch long cinnamon is Arizona's newest hummer. Our one and only record was reported from Patagonia, near Sonoita Creek, northeast of Nogales. The bird was observed at a feeder from July 21 through July 23, 1992. One was also recorded in New Mexico a year later.

The cinnamon normally occurs in the arid lowlands of western and southern Mexico, south to central Costa Rica. The bird is aptly named: its entire underparts are cinnamon. The upperparts are metallic green bronze. The tail is deep cinnamon-rufous or chestnut, tipped with bronze. The bill is reddish, tipped black. As with most members of the genus *Amazilia*, male and female are similar in appearance.

Lucifer is another 3.5-inch, 3-gram hummer. The male has a purple gorget like that of a Costa's, but lacks the Costa's violet crown. Also, the male Lucifer's immaculate white underparts have a strong buff wash on the sides and flanks that is lacking in the Costa's. The male's upperparts are greenish and his dark green tail is long, narrow, and deeply forked. The female lacks the gorget and has a bold white stripe (bordered by darker feathers below) from the eye onto the side of the neck. She also has more uniformly buff underparts, and a more rounded tail that has a strong patch of buff at the base. In both sexes, the relatively long bill is slightly but conspicuously decurved.

In the United States, the Lucifer is known only from extreme southeastern Arizona, southwestern New Mexico, and especially the Chisos Mountains of west Texas. South of the border, the breeding range of this Chihuahuan Desert species extends to south-central Mexico. It winters in Mexico.

May is a good time to look for Lucifers in Arizona. The hunt should continue through September. Lower Cave Creek Canyon in the Chiricahuas is probably the best place to look, although not to be counted on. Adventuresome souls who want to *try* to see a Lucifer away from feeders should try the south side of Joe's Canyon Trail in the Coronado National Memorial (Huachuca Mountains), from July through September. With Mexico as a backdrop, finding a Lucifer on the agave and ocotillo studded slopes there is not to be forgotten.

Costa's Hummingbird

(Calypte costae)

Photo by
G.C. Kelley

Behind the crown, the male's upperparts are standard metallic green. Below the gorget his throat is white, and the rest of the underparts greenish.

Another small hummer, Costa's measures 3 to 3.5 inches and weighs 3 grams. The male's crown and gorget are iridescent violet to violet blue. The gorget extends well back along the throat, forming almost a handle-bar style mustache. It is also solid, lacking the spackled-ray pattern of the calliope's redder gorget. Behind the crown, the male's upperparts are standard metallic green. Below the gorget, his throat is white, and the rest of the underparts greenish. The female is gray-green above, and white below. She lacks the male's vivid gorget and crown, but has a thin white line behind her eye. The bill is short and black in both sexes.

Costa's ranges from the Mohave and Great Basin deserts and chaparral-covered slopes of central California, Nevada, and southwestern Utah down through the Mohave and Sonoran deserts of Arizona into northwestern Mexico. It breeds throughout that range, but in winter withdraws from the northern parts. In Arizona, Costa's breed in the southern and western third of the state.

Of all the Arizona hummers, Costa's is most accurately described as a desert dweller. It frequents desert washes and arid slopes, and urban settings with appropriate xeric landscaping. As desert is converted to urban environments, especially well-watered ones,

Costa's are often displaced by Anna's. But if you see a hummer perched on an ocotillo on a desertscrub-covered hillside, its likely to be a Costa's. And what a sight that is, to see the sun shining on a male's gorget and crown next to the flaming orange-red of a full set of ocotillo flowers. In any event, don't count on seeing a Costa's above 3,000 to 3,500 feet.

Courtship in Costa's literally involves moving in circles. The male flies at top speed in a slightly elongated circle (vertical to the ground). After diving, he regains altitude and reaches the top again, and fades off from the circle. While displaying, he gives a "very high-pitched thin, whining whistle" that first ascends, then descends in pitch. Males also have a variety of other call notes. After a successful courtship, the male seeks a new love while the female goes on about the business of rearing a family.

Costa's nests usually occur at a height of 2 to 15 feet in low bushes or other vegetation. Most are in relatively open sites affording a good view and quick entrance or exit for the female. The outer wall of the cup-shaped nest is loosely fashioned from plant fibers held together by spiderwebs, in typical hummingbird style. The nest rim and interior are usually of small, dark feathers, affording a soft cushion for the two eggs. In Arizona, active Costa's nests have been noted from late January through early June.

Photo by
W.S. Hawk

This is a hummingbird of imposing size and intense color.

MAGNIFICENT HUMMINGBIRD

(Eugenes fulgens)

The magnificent, Arizona's second largest hummer, is 5 inches long, with a wing spread of 7 inches and a weight of 6.5 to 7.75 grams. Some field guides identify this species by its former common name, Rivoli's hummingbird. With due respect to the late Victor Massena, Duke of Rivoli, the newer common name is well chosen.

This is a hummingbird of imposing size and intense color. Males have a large iridescent green gorget and deep purple crown. The chest and belly are glossy green-black, and the wings, back, and tail are metallic dark green. The undertail coverts are grayish white. Females are emerald green above, whitish or grey to dusky green below (with speckled throat), with grayish white edges on the three outer tail feathers. Both sexes have an imposing long, black bill.

Southern Arizona and New Mexico, and southwestern Texas, represent the northern edge of the breeding distribution for this species. From here they range south to Nicaragua. In Arizona they are best known as summer residents in Cochise, Pima, and Santa Cruz counties, occasionally ranging north to the Mogollon Rim and northwest to Flagstaff, the North Kaibab Plateau, and the White Mountains. Each year, a few winter in southeastern Arizona in protected canyons where feeders are maintained. Early birds arrive in mid-March from their wintering grounds in Mexico, and head south again in October.

Magnificents prefer mountain canyons at elevations of 5,000 to 8,500 feet, with riparian woodlands of deciduous and coniferous trees. Also, expect to see them on the adjoining mountain slopes of Madrean oak-pine woodlands, mixed conifer forests, and in mountain meadows.

Magnificents drink from nectar-bearing flowers but also feed heavily on small spiders, insects, and other arthropods. They snap these "bugs" from the air or glean them from foliage while on the wing. Although not as aggressive as a blue-throat, the magnificent also contests other hummers for access to flowers or feeders. Its call note, described as a sharp *chip* or *schip*, is easily recognizable. Commensurate with its body size, its wingbeats are notably slower than those of other Arizona hummers. You can actually see its wings in flight. Or think you can.

Magnificent hummingbirds nest in tall trees in canyons and on mountain slopes. They build an erect cup on a horizontal branch, usually 30 to 50 feet above ground but as low as 10. The nest is about 2 inches across, built of spider-webs, fine plant fibers, and mosses, and decorated with lichens. The inside is lined with down and silky fibers. The average clutch is two half-inch long eggs that are incubated by the female for about 16 days. The young are fed regurgitated nectar and insects.

White-eared Hummingbird ➡️

(Hylocharis leucotis)

Photos by
Rick & Nora Bowers

Plain-capped Starthroat

(Heliomaster constantii)

The plain-cap is big by Arizona hummer standards, at 4.5 inches long and 7.25 to 7.5 grams. Its bill is the longest of any of our hummers. The male has an iridescent red gorget, bold white facial stripes, and a conspicuous streak of white on the rump. The crown is dull bronze-green. Otherwise the starthroat is metallic bronze-green above, and cloudy gray or off-white on the chest, becoming paler on the abdomen. Its tail is bronze-green basally, with a subterminal blackish band, and white tips on the outer feathers. The female has much less red, or none, on the throat, but is otherwise very similar to the male.

One of Arizona's more recent arrivals, the star-throat is common in the arid lowlands, foothills, and scrub from southern Sonora on south to Costa Rica. It was first noted here near Nogales in 1969. Now the statewide tally stands at about two dozen records, from May 20 to November 28. Most fall between June and September. A possible breeding record has been reported, from near Patagonia.

Alphabetically last but certainly not least among Arizona hummingbirds, the white-ear is 3.5 inches long and weighs less than 4 grams. The male's bright purple-blue head is violet on the crown, violet and emerald green on the throat. He has a distinctive, broad white stripe ("ear") from the eye along the side of the neck toward the shoulder. The rest of his body is metallic dark to golden green, except for a white abdomen and a violet blue ring around the base of the tail. The tail has a squared tip; the outer feathers are tipped pale. The female also has a white eye stripe, but only small flecks of color on the whitish throat. She has green flanks and white-tipped outer tail feathers. Both sexes have a relatively short red bill, tipped black.

The white-ear is common in high mountains from Mexico to Nicaragua. It may be the most common hummingbird above 5,000 feet in central and northern Mexico. Most Arizona summer records are from Ramsey Canyon, in the Huachucas. White-ears have also been seen in the Chiricahua, Santa Rita, and Santa Catalina mountains of southeastern Arizona. They also occur in southwestern New Mexico (Animas Mountains) and west Texas (Chisos Mountains).

Mountain forests of pines and oaks, and wooded canyons with flowing streams are the white-ear's favored haunts. Although quite bellicose when defending a territory, white-ears observed at feeders in Arizona are often described as "shy." They spend most of their time perched in the woods until, almost like clockwork, they flit in to sip from a feeder, only to return immediately to a relatively secluded perch.

RUFOUS HUMMINGBIRD
(Selasphorus rufus)
Photo by W.S. Hawk

At 3.5 inches and 3.5 grams, the rufous has a disposition to match a hummer twice its size. It's also arguably America's most beautiful hummer. The male has a flaming orange-red gorget, a white bib below, and the rest of its body is orange-rufous. Then there's the female: no gorget; a few spackles of red to golden green on the throat; and the rufous confined to the back, basal half of the tail feathers, and a wash on the sides and flanks. A blackish band on her tail feathers separates the rufous base from the white tips.

The rufous breeds in woodlands, gardens, and parks of southern Alaska, western Canada, Washington, Oregon, Idaho and western Montana. It winters in Mexico, south to Guererro and Veracruz. In Arizona, we know the rufous as a migrant headed north in February through May, and south in early July (males) through October. It is often abundant here at feeders in mountain canyons above 5,000 feet. Males returning south show up so early in July in Arizona that many people mistake them for breeding birds.

The male rufous' wings produce a buzz in flight, but the sound is unlike that produced by a broad-tail. The rufous' buzz is also high pitched, but quiet and, many people say, not very musical. It's another judgment call: one person's buzz is another's trill. The most common call notes are a soft *tchup*, and an "excited, buzzy squeal": *zeeee-chuppity-chub*.

ALLEN'S HUMMINGBIRD
(Selasphorus sasin)
Photo by Rick & Nora Bowers

A twin to the rufous in size and color, Allen's is probably Arizona's most over-reported hummer. The female Allen's and female rufous are practically identical. Males differ largely in the color of their back: green on the Allen's, rufous on the rufous. Or so the books would have us believe. In reality, a male Allen's may have considerable rufous on its back, and a male rufous may have a few to many bronze-green spackles on the back. So, how do you tell these species apart? Under very close and careful observation, with good binoculars and steady hands, check the outer tail feathers. On the Allen's, they are very narrow; the outer one on each side appears bristle-like. Another technique: let discretion be the better part of valor; simply record "rufous-Allen" on your checklist, and leave this issue for the "experts" to sort out. Actually, studies by Steve and Ruth Russell tell us about nine of 10 *Selasphorus* hummers banded in Arizona are of the rufous persuasion.

Allen's breed in wooded, forest-edge, and chaparral habitats, canyons, ravines, and parklands along the West Coast of the United States. In late summer and fall, most return to Mexico (some are resident in California) to winter in the central western states, including Baja California.

VIOLET-CROWNED HUMMINGBIRD

(Amazilia violiceps)

Photo by
Rob Curtis/VIREO

...the violet-crown is the fourth largest hummer native to the United States. It is also another very strong candidate for our most beautiful hummer, but because of its almost restrained elegance rather than the gaudy brilliance of the rufous hummingbird.

The violet-crown is 4 to 4.25 inches long, and weighs a hefty 5 to 5.75 grams. By American hummer standards, that is big. In fact, the violet-crown is the fourth largest hummer native to the United States. It is also another very strong candidate for our most beautiful hummer, but because of its almost restrained elegance rather than the gaudy brilliance of the rufous hummingbird. As with all *Amazilia* hummingbirds, male and female violet-crowns are similar in appearance, but the male's crown is iridescent violet-blue (purple) and the female's is duller. In both sexes, the underparts are snowy white from chin to base of tail; no other male U.S. hummer has a white throat. The back and tail feathers are gray-brown, perhaps just a bit mousy in color. Both sexes have a strong red (pink) bill that is tipped blackish (dusky).

With an extensive range in Mexico (south to Chiapas), the violet-crown barely enters the United States in west Texas, southwestern New Mexico, and southeastern Arizona. For more than 20 years it has most commonly been seen in canyons at the junction of Arizona, Sonora, and New Mexico, in a setting that becomes more beautiful with every passing year of cooperative riparian habitat recovery efforts by private and government landowners. Violet-crowns are also regular along Sonoita Creek, near Patagonia, on the south side of the Santa Rita Mountains. They also show up in the Chiricahua Mountains (e.g. Cave Creek Canyon) and in the Huachuca Mountains (several canyons). Arizona records suggest an expanding range for this species, and not just a reflection of more birders being afield and finding birds at previously undocumented sites.

Exceptionally early violet-crowns may appear in Arizona any time after February, but an April to May arrival is more dependable. They are most often seen along streams, licking (hummingbirds **don't** suck) nectar from flowers flourishing in the moist soil. They work from flower to flower, in a "traplining" sequence common among hummingbirds. By early September, most of them are gone again. Recently a few wintering birds have been noted in Arizona at feeders in Bisbee, Patagonia, and Tucson.

Violet-crown nests are placed well above ground, typically at 25 to 40 feet in a sycamore, affixed to a horizontal limb offering easy access and a good view. The first record of a violet-crown nest in the United States was reported in 1959, from Guadalupe Canyon. According to ornithologist Bill Baltosser, who has studied this species in Guadalupe and elsewhere in the United States and Mexico, the violet-crown is typically a wet season breeder. In Arizona, that means July through September.

Bats of Arizona

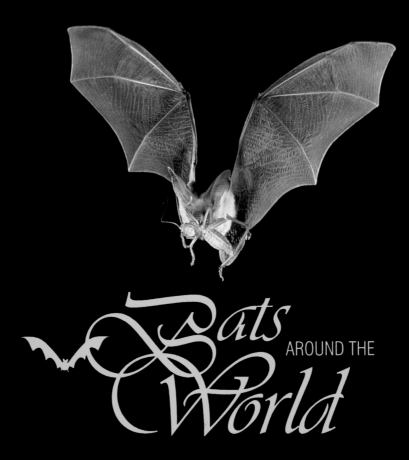

Bats AROUND THE World

Bats are unique among the world's 4,500+ species of mammals. All 900+ species fly. They don't glide, like a so-called "flying" squirrel or a "flying lemur." They fly. They provide their own power, and generally control their own flight plan. It seems such a simple step, such a positive step, that we wonder why more mammals haven't followed suit, as if they could choose an evolutionary course at will. Virtually all bats fly and most fly very well. In fact, the exceptions are so few as to be truly remarkable, whether extinct or extant. So why don't more mammals fly? Well, we don't know, so we can't tell you. But we can tell you a little something about these incredible mammals that have taken to the skies, and that's just what we hope to do in this special issue of Arizona Wildlife Views.

The ties that bind all mammals together are few, but strong. All species have hair, nurse their young, and produce their body heat internally. Other characteristics also hold true for most species, but these are the basics that distinguish all mammals from the soaring birds, earth-groveling reptiles, slimy amphibians, and scaly fishes. And bats are no exception. They have much the same basic internal structure and physiological processes as other mammals, but oh those externalities, how they do differ.

In scientific terms, all bats belong to the order Chiroptera (meaning hand-wing). The species are arranged in two suborders, the Megachiropterans (big bats), and the Microchirop-terans (small bats). But like so many scientific words and stereotypes, this scheme doesn't always hold up. The Megachiropterans include bats that are as small as most any of the "small" bats, and some Microchiropterans are pretty darn big.

Aside from vampire bats (of which there are only three species—and none in Arizona), the flying foxes of the Old World are probably the world's most famed bats. These Megachiropterans inhabit the tropics and subtropics from mainland Africa east to Australia and the equally exotic smaller Pacific islands. Among 170 species in the single family in this group are bats which have head-body lengths of 16 inches and wingspans of nearly 6 feet. That reach serves them well, as some species even fly from one island to another, in search of their prey, the elusive—fruit.

Although fox-like faces gave rise to their common name, these big bats do not eat meat. They are mainly fruit eaters, or in a few cases, insect or nectar eaters. And what's more, most of them don't find their food or navigate by echo-location, as do most bats. Their eyes are very well developed (though they lack cones, as do all bats), and visual cues are essential to their travels far and wide. Once in close range, a strong sense of smell helps locate the desired morsels.

That only leaves about 780 species of bats to account for in the 17 families comprising the Microchiroptera. Even if we just summarized the diversity within each family, we wouldn't get where we need to be in another 900 words (i.e. at an ending), so we'd better pick up on the "externalities" concept that we mentioned earlier.

The Microchiropterans occur virtually worldwide. Only very distant, small islands and the frozen, treeless north and south latitudes are bat free. At tropical latitudes, or even in some temperate climes, any given area may be inhabited by many species and/or by huge numbers of bats. In fact, in some places bats may be more numerous than all other mammals combined, with the frequent exception of rodents. Even Arizona has a hefty 28 species, but they represent only four of the Microchiropteran families: Mormoopidae, Phyllostomidae, Vespertilionidae, and Molossidae.

The "small" bats of the world have much the same skeletal characteristics as Megachiropterans. They have shortened bodies, with elongated fingers that stretch skin into "wings," thus their general body shape is also very similar. Internally, the digestive, circulatory, and nervous systems are much the same as those of other mammals, but they reflect the evolutionary changes associated with flight and a particular mode of life.

Again, the basic structures are much the same for Microchiropterans as for the big bats; they are just generally smaller in scale and there are far more species to consider. Their bodies vary from drab, mouse colors to red, yellowish, and silver. Still others have pure white stripes or spots on a jet black background; the contrast is both startling and beautiful. But ultimately, all bats have fur on their bodies, and generally naked skin across the fingers (i.e. the "wings").

The variation related to feeding strategies is amazing. Some bats have teeth and jaws adapted for eating hard-bodied insects, others for eating soft-bodied insects. In fact, some 70 percent of the bats of the world practice *insectivory*, some taking their prey on the wing and others gleaning them from the foliage.

Still others have sharp, if small, teeth and eat suitably-sized frogs, lizards, rodents, and birds (*carnivory*). There are fish-eating bats (*piscivory*) and even some bat-eating bats (cannibals)! And yes, a few species—actually three and only three—have razor sharp (but still very small) teeth and drink fresh blood (*sanguivory*). One of them feeds on mammals (primarily livestock), the other two feed on birds, and none of the three occur in Transylvania, or in Arizona, except in zoos.

Some bats are adapted to eating fruits (*frugivory*), and some have elongated tongues and reduced teeth well suited to a diet of nectar (*nectarivory*) and/or pollen. Even so, at birth all bats drink their mother's milk, and even the vampires are said to "adopt" orphaned young.

Reproductively, Microchiropteran bats are very similar to other mammals in basic structure, but the manner in which the equipment is used is remarkable. In some species, ovulation and fertilization occur after emergence from hibernation. In others, they occur before hibernation and the fertilized egg awaits spring before implantation occurs. Still others mate before hibernation, then store the sperm until after spring emergence.

In any event, most temperate latitude bats bear one young per year. Some tropical species may have two or more estrus cycles per year, but they still tend to have one young per litter, which is still an extremely slow reproductive rate for animals this small. This also makes it very difficult for bats to recover from population declines, and sometimes even to hold their own in the face of continued losses.

All things considered, the bats of the world are a keystone to the world. They are invaluable links in the web of life, and there is far more to say on their behalf than can be said here. Fortunately, interested readers can consult some resources in their public or university libraries.

Among the earlier bat books, one well worth reading as a pure adventure in science, is the classic *Listening in the Dark* (D.R. Griffin 1956). Much of Griffin's information on echolocation is dated now, but his approach to learning is worth considering regardless of your area of interest. E.P. Walker's amazing *Mammals of the World* (Fifth Edition, revised by R.M. Nowak 1991) offers excellent synopses on the bats of the world. *Bats of America* (R.W. Barbour and W.H. Davis 1969) has more detailed information for all species known from north of Mexico. *Mammals of Arizona* (D.F. Hoffmeister 1986) has excellent species accounts for Arizona's 28 bats. *Bats: a Natural History* (J.E. Hill and J.D. Smith 1984) fleshes out the discussion of evolution and diversity very nicely. All of these sources and others have been consulted in producing this issue of *Views*.

When all is said and done, though, there is likely nothing more important than transforming information into knowledge, and knowledge into protection of the world's finite resources. In the bat world, education and conservation inevitably bring us to Bat Conservation International, and Dr. Merlin D. Tuttle. Anyone can spout off facts about how many insects a colony of 10 to 20 million free-tailed bats (that existed just a few decades ago in eastern Arizona before the impacts of DDT and the like) can consume in a single night. (Answer: 500,000 pounds or 250 tons.) Anyone can tell you how likely a human is to get rabies from a bat. (Answer: less than one chance in a million.) And anyone can tell you how valuable bats are as sources of guano, pollinators of flowers, transplanters of seeds, and focal points of biomedical research. But facts don't necessarily change the way we live, or consume.

Merlin Tuttle has used facts and a sincere, straightforward approach to conservation to elevate the world's consciousness about bats, probably more than any other single person. His user-friendly book, *America's Neighborhood Bats* (1988) never lets its content get in the way of its message that bats are fascinating, bats are valuable, bats are worth saving, and you can help. So, if, as Dr. Tuttle says, "Bats are feared only to the extent that they are misunderstood," makes sense to you, a pleasant journey through his book may be the best way to begin breaking down those fears. Get a copy, and scads of other great bat information from: Bat Conservation International, P.O. Box 162603, Austin, Texas 78716. ✇

Ghost-faced bat
Mormoops megalophylla

MERLIN D. TUTTLE

Ghost-faced bats are very uncommon in Arizona. Since 1954 only two females have been collected, both in the Santa Rita Mountains on the Coronado National Forest. They were caught at 4,450 feet elevation in a mist net over a waterhole in a woodland riparian area consisting of mature cottonwood, sycamore, and willows. The nearest known colony is about 250 miles south of this Arizona netting location in Mexico. No specimens have been reported since, and nothing more is known about, its distribution in Arizona.

The species' total range extends from southern Arizona and southern Texas through Mexico, parts of Central America, and northern South America. The genus *Mormoops* prefers humid to arid and semi-arid regions, usually below 9,800 feet. Of the two species in the genus, the ghost-faced bat is the only one found in North America. The other species, the Antillean ghost-faced bat (*M. blainvillii*), is found only on some of the Caribbean Islands.

The ghost-faced bat is medium-sized (0.5 ounces), with long, loose fur that is brownish to reddish brown. It can be identified by the leaf-like folds of skin that extend from ear to ear across the chin and in front of the lower lip. In addition, the ears are connected across the forehead, forming a pocket below the eye. The end of the tail points upward from near the middle of the tail membrane. The average wingspread of this bat is 14.5 inches and the average body length is 2.5 to 3 inches. There is no other bat in the United States with these characteristics.

This bat is colonial and roosts during the day in caves and mines. Occasionally they roost in buildings and railroad tunnels. Buildings may also be used for night roosts. This species apparently does not migrate nor hibernate. They have been found in warm roosts during the winter in Texas and Mexico, indicating they remain active year-round.

Ghost-faced bats eat mainly insects that are captured in flight. They look for food high above the ground, and as a result, are rarely caught in mist nets. They are strong, fast fliers and apparently are unable to detect mist nets. Thus, when they are caught, they hit the net with great force.

The breeding period ranges from late winter to early spring. Each reproducing female gives birth to only one offspring in June. No ghost-faced bat nursery colonies have been discovered in the United States.

Little is known about the ghost-faced bat's historical or current range, if any, in Arizona. To manage this species effectively, studies of the distribution, habitat requirements, population dynamics, and life history are needed.

California leaf-nosed bat

Macrotus californicus

The California leaf-nosed bat is a rather large bat, with big ears and a "leaf" on the end of its nose. It is brown in color and its tail extends beyond the tail membrane. It has fairly large eyes and can see well. When captured and handled, this bat is reluctant to bite and does not make any sound that humans can hear. The average wingspread of this bat is 13.5 inches and the average body length is 2 to 2.5 inches.

The California leaf-nosed bat lives predominantly in Sonoran and Mohave desertscrub habitats, but is occasionally found in the Chihuahuan and Great Basin deserts. It can be found in southern California, southern Nevada, southwestern Arizona, and southward to the southern tip of Baja California, Mexico, northern Sinaloa, Mexico, and southwestern Chihuahua, Mexico. During the day, this species roosts primarily in mines and caves. At night it may rest in open buildings, cellars, bridges, porches, and mines that offer overhead protection but which are open for adequate flight approach.

California leaf-nosed bats do not hibernate like many bats, nor do they migrate. Although they may move from one roost to another, they tend to live in the same area year after year and remain active year-round. Sustained exposure to ambient temperatures of less than 78 degrees may cause death.

California leaf-nosed   RANDY BABB

Mexican long-tongued   MERLIN D. TUTTLE

Lesser long-nosed   MERLIN D. TUTTLE

Mating takes place in the fall. During the winter, the embryo develops very slowly until March, then proceeds at normal rates. Females congregate in maternity colonies to give birth to one young during May and June. The young can fly and forage on their own after one month. The maximum life expectancy for this species is 15 years or more.

California leaf-nosed bats are most active shortly after sunset and about two hours before sunrise. They primarily eat insects, including grasshoppers, cicadas, beetles, dragonflies, sphinx moths, butterflies, and caterpillars. They tend to "glean" or take insects off the ground or from the vegetation instead of catching insects in flight. They can hover well and are very agile in flight, but cannot move on the ground well or crawl like many bats. It has been suggested that this species occasionally also eats cactus fruit.

This species is quite susceptible to human disturbance, which can hinder reproduction or force individuals from a roost into the extreme daytime temperatures, especially during summer months. Loss of habitat by sealing off mine shafts and caves is also detrimental.

MERLIN D. TUTTLE

MERLIN D. TUTTLE

Family — *Phyllostomidae*

Lesser long-nosed bat

Leptonycteris curasoae

Found well into Central America, the lesser long-nosed bat occurs in Arizona from the Picacho Mountains south and west to the Agua Dulces, and south and east to the Chiricahuas, and into Mexico. It also occurs in southwestern New Mexico and Baja California. Those that summer in the United States winter in Mexico, but they do not hibernate.

The long-nosed is one of Arizona's three leaf-nosed bats. It has large eyes, the family's distinctive leaf-like flap of skin at the base of a relatively long nose, small ears, no visible tail, and a greatly reduced interfemoral membrane. It is grayish to reddish-brown above, and brown below. Wingspan averages about 14 inches. Adults average 0.7 ounces. The average body length of this bat is 2.5 to 3 inches.

They usually arrive in Arizona in mid-April. Females are already pregnant, having mated while wintering in Mexico. They soon congregate into maternity colonies, some of which once numbered in the tens of thousands. Today, the known colonies are smaller, typically a few hundred individuals at most, or fewer. The young are born in May, and can fly by the end of June. Maternity colonies break up in mid-summer. Males form smaller, separate roosting colonies.

Like the Mexican long-tongued, the lesser long-nosed feeds primarily on flower nectar and pollen. In early summer, columnar cacti such as saguaros and organpipes are favorite foraging sites. Later, agaves are sought out. In either case, pollen that collects on the hovering bat's head and shoulders as it probes one flower is soon transferred to another. At flight speeds of up to 14 mph, a long-nosed can touch a lot of flowers each night. What pollen is not transferred to flowers is ingested when the bat grooms after feeding. Pollen streaks on a roost wall or floor indicate this species' presence.

In Arizona, from April through July, females are found mostly in areas with flowering saguaros and organpipe cactus at elevations below about 3500 feet. During July their range expands as some females and young, plus some late-arriving males, move up to about 5500 feet in areas of semidesert grassland and lower oak woodland where they forage on agave blossoms. They have all left for more southerly wintering grounds by late September or early October.

In 1988, the lesser long-nosed bat was federally listed under the Endangered Species Act. More recent information suggests population declines and threats may not be as great as was believed to be the case when federal listing occurred. Roost disturbance and possible effects of habitat loss such as over-harvest of agaves in Mexico contribute to continued concern for this bat.

MERLIN D. TUTTLE

Family — *Phyllostomidae*

Mexican long-tongued bat

Choeronycteris mexicana

More widely distributed in the country from which it draws its name, the Mexican long-tongued bat occurs in Arizona from the Chiricahuas to the Santa Catalinas and Baboquivaris. It also edges into southwestern New Mexico and southern California. It winters in Mexico, but does not hibernate. Its northerly summer haunts are reserved for breeding.

The long-tongued is actually a leaf-nosed bat, one of three such species in Arizona. It has the family's distinctive leaf-like flap of skin at the tip of a relatively long and slender nose, medium-sized ears, and a tiny tail (0.4 inches, roughly one-third the length of the membrane between its legs). It is buffy brown to dark or sooty grayish-brown above, and paler below. Wingspan averages 13 to 14 inches. Adults average 0.7 ounces. The average body length of this bat is 2.5 to 3 inches.

In Arizona, these bats inhabit the oak-pine belt, mainly at elevations of 4,000 to 6,000 feet. They have also been noted in saguaro-paloverde desertscrub, but generally if a leaf-nosed species is present at lower elevations this far north, it will not be the Mexican long-tongued. Regardless of the plant community occupied, caves and abandoned mine shafts are typical roosts. The bats often hang near the entrance, in dimly lit areas that offer quick escape routes.

Though considered colonial, this species is a relative "loner." Its roosts typically include a dozen or fewer individuals, and often no other kinds of bats. It appears only pregnant females move north from Mexico in summer. Males are absent from maternity colonies, which are in full bloom from mid-June through early July, when the young are born. Females may carry the single young in flight, but within three weeks the young can fly and the colony becomes nomadic, changing roosts while searching for elysian fields of flowering agaves.

A long, bristle-like tongue and a lack of lower incisors give a hint of this species' true diet. Although insects may also be taken, its staples are nectar and pollen. They are usually collected on the wing from agaves, but even hummingbird feeders may be harvested effectively!

The Mexican long-tongued bat is not federally listed under the Endangered Species Act, but more information is needed before a knowledgeable determination can be made as to the need for federal listing. Roost disturbance and possible effects of habitat loss such as over-harvest of agaves in Mexico contribute to continued concern for this bat. ⌄

Allen's lappet-browed bat

Idionycteris phyllotis

MERLIN D. TUTTLE

Allen's lappet-browed bat is one of Arizona's five big-eared bats. It has a statewide range, except for the southwestern deserts. A relative newcomer to Arizona's bat fauna, only three specimens had been collected before 1960. Gradually more have been collected, typically in ponderosa pine, pinyon-juniper, Mexican woodland, and riparian habitats above 3,000 feet. Now this species is known from dozens of sites in six counties, including maternal roosts of up to 150 individuals. This has led some biologists to speculate that its range has recently expanded into Arizona from Mexico, for unknown reasons.

These bats are distinguished from others by their tawny fur and long ears. The latter exceed one inch in length, with lappets of skin projecting forward from their base. At rest, the huge ears are folded along the back. The wingspan is 12 to 14 inches; males are significantly larger than females. The average body length of this bat is 2 to 2.5 inches.

Often lappet-browed bats are captured in flight, along streams. People who have captured them in mist nets report that the captures are usually made several hours after sunset. This indicates the bats may feed on insects that are active later in the night. Their preferred food is small moths, but they also take beetles, roaches, and flying ants. These insects are taken in flight or gleaned from surfaces.

Lappet-browed bats are very maneuverable fliers, often hovering and flying vertically. Why such a skilled flier is so easily captured in nets seems like a reasonable question. Perhaps its tendency to fly with "swift, direct movements from one place to another, interspersed with slower flights" may give at least a partial answer.

Much of this species' life history is unknown. Only females have been found in maternal roosts, though they often share those roosts with a variety of other species of bats. The roosting habits of males remain a mystery. The young are born in June, and are flying by late July. The only hibernating colony found in Arizona to date was near Kingman, in February 1992. It held one individual.

Protection of the maternal roosts, usually in mine adits and caves, is the primary management strategy for this species until further studies have been completed.

Big brown bat
Eptesicus fuscus

The big brown bat is a medium-to large-sized bat, generally weighing 0.3 to 0.7 ounces. It is hard to confuse with other species because of its relatively large size and its tail, which extends beyond the tail membrane. Big browns also possess a broad "unornamented" nose that is quite distinctive. The average wingspread of this bat is 13 to 14 inches and the average body length is 2.5 to 3 inches.

The big brown bat ranges from Alaska and Canada south throughout most of the continental United States to northern South America, including the Caribbean Islands. In the United States the only place it does not occur includes southern

MERLIN D. TUTTLE

Florida and much of central Texas. In Arizona, the big brown bat is found throughout mid-to higher-elevation forests and at some lower elevations throughout the summer. In winter, it is found south of the Mogollon Rim.

Big brown bats are closely associated with man and are possibly familiar to more people in the United States than any other bats. In summer months they are well known for forming colonies in man-made structures, including attics, barns, churches, behind shutters, beneath bridges, tunnels, and mines. Two unique roost sites reported for this species include cliff swallow nests in Texas, and a hollow saguaro in Arizona.

The big brown bat emerges at dusk. It is known for its strong and nearly straight pattern of flight. It forages in meadows and pastures, along tree-lined streets, and beneath bright lights. It preys on a number of insects, including termites, true bugs, leaf hoppers, flying ants, and many species of beetles.

Breeding generally occurs in the fall, but has been observed through March. The female retains the sperm in her body until spring, when ovulation occurs. The young are born in small nursery colonies during the summer, and can fly within a month of birth. During late pregnancy and when the young are small, adult males are scarce at maternity roosts.

When mothers leave to forage in the evenings, all newborns are left behind. The female can locate and pick up her young, even when one or more young fall from their roost site to the floor. Scientists believe the mothers can distinguish their young from others by the constant low-frequency "squeaking" the babies emit when separated from the colony.

In late summer, big brown bats become extremely fat in preparation for hibernation. When hibernating, they tend to choose sites near a refuge entrance where temperatures are low and relative humidity is less than 100 percent.

Although threats do exist to some local populations, especially when they roost in or near structures inhabited by people, big brown bats are not of much concern to wildlife managers because they are widely distributed and appear to have relatively stable populations. ❥

Family — *Vespertilionidae*

California myotis
Myotis californicus

One of the more common bats of the desert scrub areas in Arizona, the California myotis can also be found up to the oak and ponderosa pine habitats of the state. Occurring statewide, they tend to be less common in the higher mountain areas, apparently avoiding spruce-fir forests. The known range of this myotis includes the western United States south into Mexico. Its winter distribution in Arizona includes the southernmost part of the state, below the Gila River. The average wingspread of this bat is 9 inches and the average body length is 1.5 to 2 inches.

This is the smallest myotis found in Arizona. It weighs about 0.1 ounces (a penny weighs approximately 0.09 ounces). The fur varies geographically and locally from pale buff to dark brownish black. The ears also vary in color from light to dark, but usually they are dark. This species can be easily confused with the western small-footed myotis. However, the California myotis tends to have a more abrupt forehead and a shorter thumb.

The California myotis is an opportunistic rooster. This means they roost in any convenient shelter and do not regularly return to the same place every day. Roost selection tends to be any available crevice, from rock fissures to loose tree bark. Maternity colonies are usually small and the young become self-dependent by mid-July. The single young is born usually in June. The winter roosts are generally in caves, mine tunnels, and buildings. These bats probably use man-made structures for night roosts more than any other species. They remain fairly active in their wintering areas and probably hibernate only as conditions demand.

The California myotis feeds in the early evening foraging in or below the canopy while searching for flying insects. When feeding near water courses, this species tends to fly over or close to the banks, in contrast to the Yuma myotis, which forages over open water. Peak activity for these bats occurs within a few hours after sunset.

The California myotis appears to be one of the more stable species of bats in Arizona. This may be due to its ability to roost in a variety of shelters without having to return to the same roost everyday. Disturbance of roosts (especially hibernating colonies) is probably the greatest threat. Winter roost surveys and determination of migrational paths should be conducted to better understand the California myotis. ✎

J. SCOTT ALTENBACH

Family — *Vespertilionidae*

Fringed myotis
Myotis thysanodes

A fringe of small hairs along the free edge of the tail membrane distinguishes this bat from any other in Arizona. This fringe, visible to the naked eye, is also the source for this species' common name. The ears are slightly shorter and this species is slightly larger than the southwestern and long-eared myotis bats. The average wing-spread of this bat is 10.5 to 12 inches and the average body length is 1.5 to 2 inches.

The fringed myotis occurs throughout western North America, from Canada south to southern Mexico. It is found in a variety of habitats from low deserts and grasslands, to ponderosa pine and spruce-fir forests. In Arizona during the summer, it is widespread except for the southwestern part of the state. It seems to prefer oak woodland, from which it forages out into nearby habitats including low desert, chaparral, and ponderosa pine. In winter, it is found in the mountains of the northwest and southeast corners of the state.

Breeding takes place in fall, but fertilization and development do not occur until early spring. Sexes roost separately during summer, with females forming maternity roosts and males segregated elsewhere. While these bats seem easily disturbed by human presence at any time, females are especially secretive and skittish prior to giving birth.

One young is born in June or July. It is capable of sustained flight and is indistinguishable from adults 21 days after birth. Within maternity roosts, females may change locations periodically. In buildings these movements seem to be associated with temperature regulation. When a nonflying young falls to the floor and is unable to climb back up the wall, an adult female might fly to the youngster in response to its distress call. The female may allow the young bat to attach to her nipple and return it to the cluster.

These bats roost in tight clusters in the open within caves, mines, and buildings which they may use for either day or night roosts. At night most fringed myotis leave the roost within one or two hours after sunset, although there may be some activity during most of the night.

Like the long-eared and Southwestern myotis, these bats are capable of slow, highly maneuverable flight and pick insect prey off the surfaces of vegetation. It has been suggested that they may even land on the ground to take prey. They seem to prefer beetles.

The fringed myotis is widespread in appropriate habitat and may sometimes be common locally. ⌄

Family — *Vespertilionidae*

Hoary bat

Lasiurus cinereus

A swift, direct flight style distinguishes this large bat from most others found in Arizona. Pointed wings with a spread of 16 inches and a heavily furred body also aid in identification. The soft fur coat is made up of dark brown hairs, many of which have white tips. These white tips give the bat a frosted or "hoary" appearance. Rounded, black-edged ears and large teeth accent its tan face and throat. The average body length of this bat is 3 to 3.5 inches.

The hoary bat is not a cave dweller but instead roosts in trees. Its days are spent hanging 10 to 15 feet above ground in the foliage of trees. This raised roosting spot keeps the bat safe from predators on the ground. The leaves of the tree hide it from owls and hawks flying above. Hoary bats occasionally fly during the day but usually do not become active until after sunset. They spend much of the night flying over clearings and open water feeding on insects. Moths appear to be their main source of food, but they also feed on beetles, wasps, grasshoppers, dragonflies, and other species of small bats.

Young hoary bats are left in their roost, hanging to a leaf or twig while their mother searches for food throughout the night. The mother returns before sunrise to spend the day in the roost with up to four babies clinging to her. The litter size is most often two. Blind and furry, the babies are born in the same tree that they will live in until they are able to fly. During this time, if the female accidentally falls from her roost she will not be able to return because of the weight of her attached young.

Summer is the best season to spot a hoary bat. They can be found in most wooded areas throughout Arizona. Hoary bats have been observed north of the tree line in Canada, and south to Chile and Argentina. Alaska is the only state in the United States where a hoary bat has not been found. A large wingspan and good flying ability have helped this bat expand its range across the Pacific Ocean to Hawaii. The hoary bat holds the honor of being the only nonmarine mammal native to the Islands of Hawaii.

The hoary bat may migrate south to wintering roosts, but no specific migration patterns or roost sites have been documented. Further investigation into its winter activities is needed, as hoary bat populations should continue to be monitored.

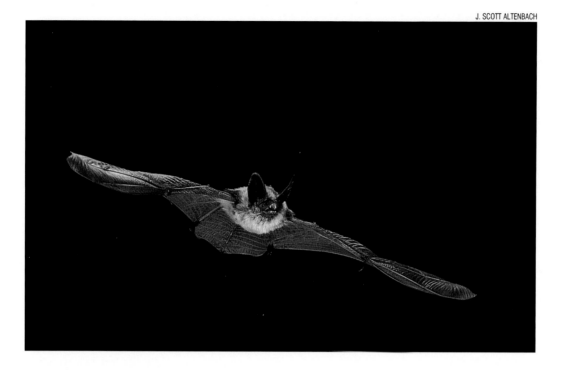

Family — *Vespertilionidae*

Long-eared myotis

Myotis evotis

With its narrow, dark-colored ears, the long-eared myotis is well named. Its ears, at nearly an inch from base to tip, average longer than those of any of the other 88 kinds of myotis bats in the world, including the other eight found in Arizona. Medium-sized and brownish, it weighs less than 0.25 ounce, spreads its wings to a span of about 10 inches, and has an average body length of 1.5 to 2 inches.

During summer months, this bat is found in forested areas throughout temperate parts of western North America, including Baja California. In Arizona during the summer, it is found on the Mogollon Rim and the Kaibab Plateau, where it occurs in conifer forests, including ponderosa pine and spruce-fir.

Interestingly, nothing is known about this bat's migration or winter habits and whereabouts in Arizona or elsewhere. It is presumed to hibernate and probably migrates short distances from its summer range to caves or abandoned mines in which it spends the winter.

Long-eared myotis roost in small groups: 12 to 30 have been found together in Canada. Day roosts may include buildings, caves, mines, hollow trees,

cracks in cliffs, sinkholes, or behind slabs of bark. Caves have been used for night roosts. In one instance in Idaho, these bats were found roosting in a lava tube with Townsend's big-eared bats.

Males and females roost separately in summer. Female long-eared myotis congregate in small groups and give birth to one young, probably in late June or early July. Nothing is known about how old the young are when they begin to fly, or when they are weaned. One male long-eared myotis was documented to have lived for 22 years.

This bat species and two others, the southwestern myotis and the fringed myotis, commonly forage for insects in the same way. They hover or fly slowly over the surface of vegetation, tree trunks, rocks, or the ground and glean or pick insects from the surface. Long-eared myotis eat many kinds of insects, the most important being soft-bodied moths.

The long-eared myotis appears to be widespread and occurs regularly, if not always commonly, in appropriate habitat. ❧

Long-legged myotis
Myotis volans

The long-legged myotis ranges throughout western North America. It has been observed as far north as Alaska and south to central Mexico. Its most easterly range extends to the Dakotas and Nebraska. In Arizona, the long-legged myotis occurs in the pinon-juniper, oak, and coniferous forests throughout the northern, central, and southeastern portions of the state. It has been observed at elevations as low as 4,000 feet to over 9,000 feet. This species does not occur in the deserts or desert mountains of southwestern Arizona.

The long-legged myotis is the only large western myotis with a well-developed keel on the calcar, a bony spur that articulates with the heel and helps support the flight membrane. Another characteristic feature of this species is that it is the only brown bat with belly fur that extends onto the underwing along an imaginary line joining the elbow and the knee. The average wingspread of this bat is 10 to 10.5 inches and the average body length is 2 to 2.5 inches.

As for many species of bats, copulation may occur in August, with the sperm being stored during winter in the female's reproductive tract. Ovulation occurs sometime between March and May, with birth occurring between May and August.

Throughout much of its range the long-legged myotis forms summer maternity colonies in buildings, rock crevices, cliffs, and trees. These bats have also been observed underneath loose bark on trees. Although this species does not use caves for roosting during the day, biologists have observed them using caves as shelters during the night. It is believed that they most often roost solitarily. In contrast, little is known about the winter habitats of the long-legged myotis. Apparently, the adults and young leave their maternity colonies in the fall, but their subsequent movements remain a mystery.

The long-legged myotis emerges in the early evening when it is still light to forage. The bats may be active throughout the night, but usually have a peak of activity during the three or four hours following sunset. In many areas they are known to be associated with water, often being observed flying 10 to 15 feet over ponds, streams, water tanks, and open meadows. They have also been observed foraging in forest openings. These bats are believed to feed primarily on moths. As the evening progresses they have a tendency to forage closer to the ground.

The long-legged myotis occurs in coniferous forests in Arizona, so some scientists are concerned that current forest management practices may impact the species. ❥

J. SCOTT ALTENBACH

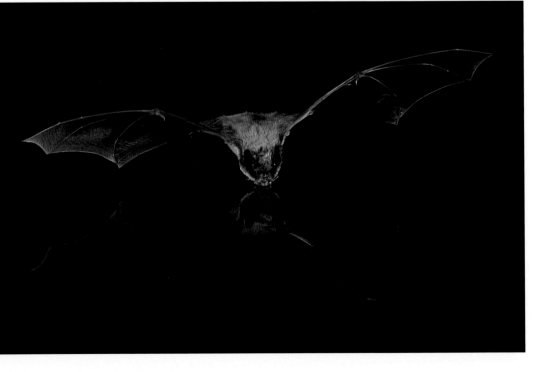

J. SCOTT ALTENBACH

Family — *Vespertilionidae*

Occult little brown bat
Myotis lucifugus occultus

This medium-sized bat is one of nine species in Arizona of the genus *Myotis*. It has sleek glossy fur, small ears, large feet, and often a bright tawny color. These traits are in addition to the typical *Myotis* characteristics of uniform coloration, the lack of a leaf-nose, a tail extending beyond the tail membrane, or fur on the tail membrane. The average wingspread of this bat is 9.5 to 11 inches and the average body length is 1.5 to 2 inches.

Most Arizona records show this species occur from the Mogollon Rim from Alpine northwest to near Flagstaff, including Mingus Mountain, Verde Valley, Sierra Ancha Mountains, and the Pinal Mountains. It likely occurs along the lower Colorado River Valley. In summer it is usually found in ponderosa pine and oak-pine woodland near water, or in riparian forests in some desert areas. Colonies have been found in buildings and in crevices between timbers of a highway bridge.

Few winter roosts are known, and no hibernating roosts are known for Arizona. Mines seem to be rarely used in summer, but some winter records are from mines. This bat is most common at higher elevations between approximately 6,000 and 9,000 feet, with some records from much lower elevations between 150 and 1,000 feet along the lower Colorado River.

Although one of the better studied species of bats, reproduction information is poor. Apparently, the sexes roost separately in summer, and known maternity colonies occur in buildings near permanent water. Apparently these bats have one young per year in late June. The young are able to fly by their third week when weaning takes place. The nursery colonies of little brown bats in other areas begin to disperse in mid-summer. At this time, young may be found in a wide variety of roosts, including sites where none had roosted previously and sometimes even in the open. Maternity colonies in the Southwest range from about 60 to 800 females. Studies on these bats in other states indicate a maximum life span of over 31 years.

This species generally hunts low over water for flying insects, probably including mosquitoes and midges. It may also eat a great variety of other insects including moths. In the Southwest, it has been observed foraging under large cottonwoods and in low elevation orchards. At higher elevations they usually forage at low levels over and around water.

The occult little brown bat may be susceptible to threats because of its limited distribution, and because the few known maternity roosts are vulnerable to disturbance. Actions needed to ensure the continued presence of this bat in Arizona include conducting surveys for maternity and hibernation roosts, thus increasing general knowledge and expanding the management options for conservation actions.

Pallid bat
Antrozous pallidus

J. SCOTT ALTENBACH

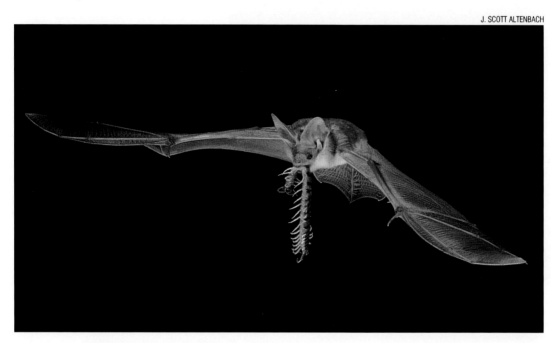

Pallid bats occur from central Mexico north through California, extending into Washington and British Columbia. In the Southwest, they are among the most common bats found at lower elevations throughout Arizona and New Mexico, and portions of Colorado, Utah, and Texas. In Arizona they frequent desertscrub habitats, and are less often in forested oak and pine regions. They prefer areas with rocky outcrops. Rarely are they found above 6,000 feet.

These beautiful bats have large ears and eyes, a distinctive snout, and pale fur that is creamy white below and light yellow with dark tips above. Odor-producing glands on the muzzle give them a "skunk-like" scent. Adults weigh just under an ounce and have a wingspan of 14 to 15 inches; females are somewhat larger than males. The average body length of this bat is 2.5 to 3 inches.

Pallid bats have a unique approach to feeding. They listen for the low frequency sounds made by ground-dwelling insects. They fly close to the ground, often alighting on the ground or on trees to capture their prey. They thoroughly chew their food, feasting on such delicious morsels as grasshoppers, June bugs, potato beetles—even scorpions!

A colonial species, the pallid bat roosts in groups of up to 100 individuals. During the summer, they are especially active and have both a daytime and nighttime roost. Night roosts are chosen for easy access and are often in open areas, such as porches, bridges, and open buildings. During the day, the bats retreat out of sight, wedging themselves into a crevice of a cliff or a building, where they may rest without disturbance. Pallid bats are prone to leaving a roost site when disturbed, or in response to extreme temperatures. Unfortunately, leaving their day roost makes them highly vulnerable to predation by hawks.

Little is known about this species' winter habits. It apparently migrates only a short distance to where it is believed to hibernate. Mating occurs throughout the winter months, but the female stores the sperm until she produces eggs in the spring.

The young are born in nursery colonies in the spring, all at about the same time. During birth, the female hangs upright and delivers the young into a "basket" formed by the tail membrane.

More information on winter roosts and habits would help manage this species more effectively.

Family — *Vespertilionidae*

Silver-haired bat

Lasionycteris noctivagans

The silver-haired bat is found throughout North America, from southeastern Alaska southward into Mexico. In Arizona, it occurs in the eastern part of the state, mainly in the higher mountains. It may be a summer resident in the northern part of the state and a year-round resident in southeastern Arizona.

Of medium size, it is dark-brown to black in color with silver or white frosting on the back, giving a salt and pepper appearance. The wingspan is 10 to 12 inches. Adults weigh 0.2 to 0.5 ounces with a body length of approximately 2 to 2.5 inches. This bat has been reported to make audible sounds under stress, ranging from a high-pitched persistent call produced by a newborn to a "sharp raspy buzzy cry" and a "high pitched bird-like peepy note" produced by adults.

Feeding on many different species of insects and spiders, these bats are extremely valuable as a natural pest control. They are believed to begin foraging about two to four hours after sunset, with a second peak of activity six to eight hours after sunset. Each individual has its own feeding route, covering from 55 to 109 square yards. They fly fairly slowly and deliberately, twisting and gliding along an erratic course in search of food.

These bats apparently roost under the bark or in crevices of large broad-leafed and coniferous trees along riparian areas and ponds. However, they have also been known to roost in wood piles, sheds, and garages. They migrate south in winter to hibernate in skyscrapers, warehouses, ship hulls, and trees. They have a lifespan of at least 12 years, even in the face of predation by owls, their principal predator.

Mating usually occurs in late September. Sperm is stored by the female during the winter. Ovulation usually occurs in late April and early May, with two young born hairless with closed eyes in June or July, after a 50-to 60-day gestation period.

At the beginning of this century, this species was regarded as common in various parts of the United States, but populations varied widely from year to year in all known localities. There is some concern for the future of the southwestern populations, due to loss of riparian forests they occupy. Little is actually known about this bat. Further study is needed to determine the actual numbers of silver-haired bats, as well as their natural history, so appropriate management and conservation plans can be established. ▼

Western yellow bat
Lasiurus xanthinus

MERLIN D. TUTTLE

The western yellow bat occurs from Uruguay and Argentina in South America, north through Central America and Mexico, into the southwestern United States. In Arizona, it is primarily known from Phoenix and Tucson, but it is thought to occur year-round throughout southern Arizona. The average wingspread of this bat is 13 to 14 inches and the average body length is 2.5 to 3 inches.

Not much is known of the habitat needs of western yellow bats, but they are usually found near thick vegetation, which they use for roosting. When found in urban areas, they are usually associated with palm trees. Ground crews trimming dead fronds from palm trees have been a major source of western yellow bat specimens. In more natural settings, western yellow bats are found in low- to mid-elevations in riparian areas which have thick, leafy vegetation.

Very little is known about the feeding habits of western yellow bats beyond the fact that they eat night-flying insects. They have been observed flying in straight lines with slow wing beats about 75 feet above the ground.

Western yellow bats give birth to one or two young in June. Like their relatives, the hoary and the red bat, yellow bats have two pairs of mammae instead of the single pair found in most bats. So far, there have been no pregnant or lactating female western yellow bats captured in Arizona, although pregnant bats have been captured just over the New Mexico border, in Guadalupe Canyon.

Possible threats are difficult to assess, since little is known of the yellow bat's biology, but may include destruction of riparian forest and woodland habitat, trimming of urban palm trees, and vandalism (burning of native palm trees). However, some biologists suggest that since there are no records for the western yellow bat prior to 1960, the bat is actually expanding its range into the United States from Mexico, aided by the wide use of ornamental palm trees in urban landscaping. Unfortunately, until more research is conducted on the distribution and biology of this species, there will be more questions than answers.

Family — *Vespertilionidae*

Southwestern cave myotis
Myotis velifer brevis

The southwestern cave myotis is one of nine Arizona bats that look very much alike. It is small and brown, with fairly small ears and no distinguishing characteristics except a sparsely furred spot between the shoulder blades. The average wingspread of this bat is 11 to 12 inches and the average body length is 2 to 2.5 inches. Its range includes the southwestern half of Arizona (except the extreme southwestern corner), and adjacent areas of California, Nevada, New Mexico, and Sonora, Mexico. During the winter, small numbers are found in southeastern Arizona.

This species roosts near water in caves, mines, barns, buildings, under bridges, and sometimes in abandoned swallow nests. They are usually located in desertscrub habitats which include creosote, brittlebush, paloverde, and cacti. Occasionally, roosts are found in pine-oak vegetation. The species is very colonial, apparently returning to the same roost every year.

Every evening, the bats fly a short distance from the roost and then return. As darkness increases, they fly a bit farther from the roost each time before returning. About 40 minutes after sunset, they finally leave the roost for the night and fly to water to drink. Afterwards, they forage just above the vegetation on such delicacies as moths, weevils, antlions, small beetles, and flying ants.

Mating occurs during the fall, but the young are not born until summer because of delayed fertilization. Males migrate north as early as March to form bachelor colonies of up to 100 individuals. The pregnant females arrive in May to form maternity colonies of 50 to 15,000 bats. A single young is born in late June to early July, after a 45- to 55-day gestation period. Although the babies remain in the roost while the females feed, they will carry their young to safety if disturbed. The young are able to fly and forage on their own in six to eight weeks. Studies indicate that adults may live up to six years, possibly up to 10 or 12 years.

During the summer and into the fall, southwestern cave myotis store fat to prepare for migration and hibernation. During hibernation, they lose 16 to 25 percent of their body weight. The hibernating roost must be cold and humid, preferably 46 to 52 degrees and above 55 percent relative humidity. The cold temperature lowers the bat's metabolism, thus requiring minimal energy for nourishment through the winter.

Because the southwestern cave myotis congregates in large groups, it is susceptible to human disturbance and encroachment. Further discovery of summer and hibernating colonies is essential, and careful management can likely prevent the need for listing this species as threatened or endangered. ᐯ

Southwestern myotis
Myotis auriculus

J. SCOTT ALTENBACH

Southwestern myotis are most similar to the long-eared myotis. Although the ears are shorter, this is not obvious without comparing measurements or individuals of both species. The most useful difference is the color of the ear and the wing membrane color; they are light-colored or browner in the southwestern myotis, and darker to blackish in the long-eared myotis. The average wingspread of this bat is 10.5 inches and the average body length is 2 inches.

Although their ranges overlap along the Mogollon Rim in Arizona and in New Mexico, the southwestern myotis is found mostly south of this area into central Mexico, with an apparently isolated population in the mountains of Guatemala. The long-eared myotis is found mostly north of this area. In Arizona and New Mexico, the southwestern myotis occurs mostly in isolated ponderosa pine forests on mountain islands of the central and southern parts of these two states. This species has also been found in ponderosa pine-mixed conifer forest, oak-pine forest, oak woodland, chaparral, and riparian forests.

This bat (like the long-eared myotis) appears to be a summer resident in Arizona and New Mexico. Although it has been captured twice in winter in southeastern Arizona, nothing else is known about its winter activities. Several records suggest that the single young is born in late June or early July. Foraging patterns are similar to those of the long-eared and the fringed myotis in which the bat hovers or flies slowly over the surface of vegetation, tree trunks, rocks, or the ground and picks insects from the surface. These three bats differ from the other six species of myotis in Arizona which forage by skimming insects over water or pursuing insects in the open air. Hovering and gleaning myotis bats, such as the long-eared myotis, have larger brains and a different style of echolocation which allows them to find insects more easily among tangled vegetation.

Insect prey (especially soft-bodied moths) for the southwestern myotis are also similar to those of the long-earned myotis, where the two are not found together. But when found together, the species change their food habits somewhat: the long-eared myotis prefers beetles and the southwestern myotis retains its preference for moths.

The southwestern myotis appears to be widespread, and occurs regularly, if not commonly, in suitable habitats. It is important to remember that distributions and populations of colonial bats are determined by availability of secure roost sites. Thus, since roost sites, especially maternity and hibernation, are vulnerable to disturbance or destruction, they must be protected. It is also important to continue learning the life history of the southwestern myotis, especially its winter activities, so we can more thoroughly evaluate its status, identify threats if any, and determine how to maintain healthy populations.

MERLIN D. TUTTLE PHOTOS

Family — *Vespertilionidae*

Spotted bat
Euderma maculatum

Of all the bats found in Arizona, the spotted bat is probably the easiest to identify. As its name implies, this bat has spots: three large white spots on a dark-colored back, one on each shoulder and one at the base of the tail. The circular bare throat patch is also distinctive. This striking pattern is enhanced by long pinkish-red ears (nearly two inches long, the largest of any North American bat). The ears are curled back at rest, but erect and pointing forward when alert and flying. The average body length of this bat is 2.5 inches.

The spotted bat is found throughout centralwestern North America, from British Columbia and Montana south through California, Texas, Utah, and into Mexico. It has been found from low desert areas in southwestern Arizona to high desert and riparian habitats in the northwestern part of the state. It has also been found in conifer forests in northern Arizona and other western states.

Roost site characteristics are poorly known for this species, but limited observations suggest that spotted bats roost singly in crevices, with rocky cliffs and surface water characteristic of localities where they occur.

The spotted bat hunts tympanate moths by using echolocation calls which are audible to humans, but at a range too low in frequency for detection by the moths. These moths have evolved thoracic "ears" which enable them to detect higher frequency echolocation calls of other insectivorous bats, but not the call of the spotted bat. The spotted bat has little difficulty taking off from the ground, thus allowing it to take other prey items such as June bugs and sometimes grasshoppers from the ground.

Reproduction is poorly understood. It appears that the spotted bat breeds in the early spring (late February to April). Limited observations indicate one young is born per female per year. Observations outside Arizona suggest young are born from late May to early July.

Initially thought to be extremely rare, the spotted bat is now known to occupy a wider range than originally believed. Increasing numbers of field workers focusing on this species are slowly improving our understanding, although population abundance and densities are still poorly known.

Townsend's big-eared bat

Corynorhinus townsendii

MERLIN D. TUTTLE

Townsend's big-eared bat is a medium-sized bat with very large ears—as much as an inch long. It also has two large lumps on the surface of the nose. It is brown in color, varying from dark brown to nearly black in more humid areas, to pale brown in the more dry, desert areas of its range. The average wingspread of this bat is 11.5 to 12.5 inches and the average body length is 2 to 2.5 inches.

This species has a very broad distribution. It is found in western North America from Washington and Wyoming east to the Black Hills of South Dakota, southward to Texas, California, Arizona, and through the Mexican uplands in southern Mexico. Isolated populations also exist in the Ozark Mountains of Oklahoma, Missouri, Arkansas, Kentucky, Virginia, and West Virginia. It

occupies a variety of habitats including deserts, woodland, and pine forests. In Arizona it is widespread, although not common anywhere. It is most uncommon in the northeastern grasslands and southwestern desert areas of Arizona.

Townsend's big-eared bats hang from open ceilings of mines and caves during the day. They do not use cracks or crevices, and may use open abandoned buildings as a night roost. In Arizona, they hibernate during the winter in cold caves, lava tubes, and mines mostly in uplands and mountains from the vicinity of the Grand Canyon to the southeastern part of the state, south of the Mogollon Rim.

These bats feed primarily on small moths. They have also been reported to take prey from vegetation while in flight. They forage in darkness, and are rarely seen at dusk. Following a late night peak of foraging activity, they usually rest in a night roost. They may also feed again shortly before dawn.

Mating occurs in October but delayed fertilization postpones the birth of one young until June. The females congregate in maternity colonies of 12 to several hundred individuals in the spring and summer, whereas the males tend to be more solitary. The young can fly at one month of age, but are not weaned until they are two months old.

Townsend's big-eared bat populations in many states are known to be declining, most notably in Oregon, Washington, and some of the eastern isolated populations in Virginia and West Virginia. This bat is highly susceptible to disturbance. Cave exploring and other recreational activities by humans have caused nursing colonies of females to abandon the roost, leaving the young to starve. Surveys designed to locate and monitor maternity colonies in Arizona are needed. ⌵

Western pipistrelle
Pipistrellus hesperus

MERLIN D. TUTTLE

In the spring and summer, just before sunset, the skies become filled with the quick turns and erratic flight of Arizona's smallest bat. The western pipistrelle is one of the most recognizable bats that live and travel within our state. It looks much like a butterfly in flight, as it flutters down canyon walls and streambeds to the open flats and bajadas of the upper desert. The average wingspread of this bat is 7.5 to 8.5 inches and the average body length is 1.5 to 2 inches.

Western pipistrelles are known throughout most of the southwestern states, from southeastern Colorado to the Pacific Ocean, and from extreme southern Washington to Mexico. In Arizona, they can be found in all types of habitats scattered throughout the state, except for the northeastern corner. During the fall, they migrate to southern Arizona or to northwestern Mohave County.

Western pipistrelles are usually found roosting in small rock crevices, but they will also use mines, caves, and buildings. They are the first bats to be seen in the evening, leaving their roost just before sunset. Their diet consists of leaf hoppers, flying ants, moths, and other insects that swarm in the warm nights. Water is never far from their day roost and is generally their first stop on their way to hunt food. The watering hole also provides prime hunting for the western pipistrelle.

These bats usually have full stomachs after about 30 minutes of foraging, and will then roost in trees and large bushes throughout the night until ready to hunt again. As the first rays of sun hit the desert, they are often seen flying for one last drink before heading back to the canyon walls to find another crevice to squeeze into.

During the early summer months, females may be found in maternity colonies of up to a dozen individuals, or alone among the rocks and canyon walls. Mating apparently occurs from September through March. The female usually gives birth to two young in June. For about a week, the young travel attached to their mother while she forages. Around the second week the young are left at the day roost. They are ready to fly alone by the fourth week.

Although western pipistrelles have been caught in mist nets during the winter, they apparently have the ability to hibernate. Nighttime temperatures probably determine if these bats emerge to forage or remain in torpor. If the female is disturbed while hibernating, she may empty the sperm she is holding. Therefore, late winter or early spring matings may be essential to guarantee reproduction.

The western pipistrelle population in Arizona appears to be stable, or at least no local declines have been reported. However, very little is known about their maternity roosts, winter habits, or migration corridors. Netting information would probably be needed to determine population trends, as searching for specific crevice roosts is almost impossible. ⌄

MERLIN D. TUTTLE PHOTOS

Family — *Vespertilionidae*

Western red bat
Lasiurus blossevillii

The Western red bat is arguably the most attractive of Arizona's bats. Its colors range from bright orange to yellow-brown, with white tipped hairs. As in songbirds, males are usually more brightly colored than females. Red bats are medium-sized bats, with a wing span of 11 to 13 inches, weighing 0.2 to 0.5 ounces, and a body length of approximately 2 to 2.5 inches.

Red bats have the broadest distribution of any American bat, ranging from extreme southern Canada through the United States east and west of the Great Plains, and south to Panama and South America. In Arizona, the red bat is thought to be a summer resident only. It occurs statewide, except in desert areas, but primarily along waterways in the central and southeastern parts of the state. The red bat has been poorly studied in Arizona. Most of what is known has been gathered from a closely related eastern species of red bat.

While red bats occasionally roost in saguaro boots and other cavities, they are more typically found roosting in dense clumps of foliage in riparian or other wooded areas. Roost sites are shaded above and tend to be open below, permitting the bats to drop into flight. When roosting, the red bat often wraps itself in its furred tail membrane and hangs from a branch by one or both feet. In this position, the bat so resembles a dead leaf or fruit that one surprised person grabbed a

female bat and her three babies in an attempt to pick what was assumed to be a peach!

Red bats emerge to forage one to two hours after dark and may forage well into the morning. They feed mainly upon flying insects and are quite willing to feed on those attracted to city street lights and the floodlights on barns. They feed to a much lesser extent on ground-dwelling insects, such as crickets.

Red bats are generally solitary, although they sometimes migrate in groups and may forage in close association with others. Copulation occurs in August and October and may be initiated in flight. The female stores the sperm until the following spring when fertilization occurs. Red bats have from one to five young per litter. With an average litter of 2.3, this is more than any other bat.

Long-term population declines are suspected for the red bat, but have not been documented. The chief threats in Arizona are its apparently low numbers and the loss of riparian and other broad-leafed deciduous forests and woodlands. ▼

Western small-footed myotis
Myotis ciliolabrum

Western small-footed myotis, once considered a subspecies of the eastern small-footed myotis *(Myotis leibii)*, can be found throughout most of Arizona with the exception of the southwestern corner. They have been found living among the oak, juniper, chaparral, and riparian areas of our state. The geographic range of the western small-footed myotis encompasses a large portion of western North America, (from southwestern Canada, spreading south to upper Baja California and western Oklahoma, and then extending south to Coahuila and Zacatecas, Mexico).

Habitat requirements for roost selection are poorly known for this species. In the summer, these bats can be found roosting in rock crevices, buildings, caves, mine tunnels, and even in loose tree bark. Unlike other small bats, they can tolerate colder and dryer hibernating areas. They have been found wintering in two areas of Arizona, south of the Gila River and in Mohave County.

The western small-footed myotis mates in the fall. The female retains the sperm until fertilization takes place in the spring. A single baby is born per year, with the birth taking place from late May to early July. Maternity colonies appear to be small, containing up to 20 individual females with young. These maternity colonies have been found in buildings and tree cavities.

These bats are insectivorous. Their diet includes moths, flies, ants, and flying beetles, which are captured while in flight.

The western small-footed myotis could benefit from a number of conservation measures. Surveying for maternity and hibernation roosts, monitoring of present and new roost sites, and determination of migratory routes are a few of the recommended measures.

The biggest threat to this species, like that of other bats, continues to be disturbance of roost sites. Just walking into a maternity colony may cause the female to drop her young. Frequent disturbances may cause the entire colony to abandon the roost.

J. SCOTT ALTENBACH

Like their name implies, these small bats have tiny feet, usually measuring about 0.3 inches. The glossy fur of this species varies from blond to dark brown. They also have dark ears and a black facial mask that aids in identification. The average wingspread of this bat is 8 to 10 inches and the average body length is 1.5 to 2 inches. The western small-footed myotis looks very similar to the California myotis, however, the small-footed bat has a flatter forehead and a longer thumb.

Family — *Vespertilionidae*

Yuma myotis

Myotis yumanensis

Have you ever seen bats flying close to the surface of a pond or lake? Chances are you were observing the Yuma myotis as it foraged over the water in search of moths, midges, caddis flies, or some other flying insect. It is one of two bats in Arizona that prefer to forage over open water, most of the time flying within a few inches of the surface. It also tends to be lunar phobic, meaning that it remains in the roost or flies in the shadows to avoid the bright moonlight. This may be a means of avoiding predation by owls.

This species can be found throughout Arizona, except for the northeastern corner. It has been found in desert, grassland, woodland, and riparian communities, but appears to be absent from the higher boreal forests of our state. The range of the Yuma myotis is from British Columbia south to Mexico. The east-west distribution appears to be from Oklahoma and Texas to coastal California. These bats are known to winter along the Lower Colorado River in Arizona.

The Yuma myotis is a small bat with relatively large feet. It is the smallest of the large-footed myotis bats. It has buffy brown fur and light colored ears with white or buff underparts. The average wingspread of this bat is 9.25 inches and the average body length is 1.5 to 2 inches.

Rarely roosting in mines or caves, these bats prefer to inhabit buildings or bridges. They are known on occasion to roost in the abandoned mud nests of cliff swallows. Like most other bats, Yuma myotis mate in the fall, with fertilization occurring in the spring. The females congregate in small maternity colonies consisting of about 35 individuals. Birth occurs from late May into June, with a single young being born. Most of the young are able to fly by early July. The adult males usually roost singly during the maternity season.

Because of its dependence on permanent water courses, the Yuma myotis may be threatened by some of the same factors that are causing declines in riparian areas in Arizona. Loss of adequate roosting sites along these water courses, and continued disturbances by people, pose threats to this species. Although population trends appear stable at this time, management efforts need to concentrate on surveying for maternity and possible hibernation roosts, finding migration routes, and monitoring known roosts. ▼

Big free-tailed bat
Nyctinomops macrotis

J. SCOTT ALTENBACH

This rather large free-tailed bat has large "bonnet" ears that extend beyond the nose when laid forward. It is found from northern South America and the Caribbean Islands northward into the western United States. In the fall, these bats apparently migrate to southern Arizona and Mexico. They are widely scattered throughout Arizona during the spring and summer. These bats have long, pointed wings and are strong flyers, capable of traveling hundreds of miles from what we think is their normal range. They have been found as far from the western United States as Iowa and British Columbia. The average wingspread of this bat is 16.5 to 17 inches and the average body length is 3 to 3.5 inches.

In Arizona, these bats have been captured in a variety of habitats including ponderosa pine, pinyon-juniper, Douglas-fir, and Sonoran desertscrub. However, it is suspected that many of these locations represent foraging locations only.

These bats apparently prefer to roost in rugged, rocky areas in desertscrub. This type of vegetation includes saguaro, creosote bush, blackbrush, sandsage, snakeweed, mesquite, and rabbitbrush.

Although much remains to be learned about its specific habitat requirements, the big free-tailed bat apparently roosts in rock crevices and fissures of mountain cliffs. By setting mist nets over water sources, biologists have concluded that this species is locally abundant, but absent from many areas with apparently suitable habitat. In addition, their abundance can change drastically over a short period of time. For instance, during the summer of 1955, researchers captured 56 big free-tailed bats at the Southwestern Research Station in the Chiricahua Mountains at Portal, Arizona. Three years later, only three of these bats were captured at the same location during the summer months.

Big free-tailed bats leave their roost in small groups relatively late in the evening to forage on large moths, crickets, flying ants, and grasshoppers. While foraging, they can emit a loud, piercing chatter, which is within the range of human hearing.

Females have one young per year, usually born in June or July. When or where breeding occurs is unknown. The only probable maternity roost was located in Big Bend National Park in 1937, in a long crevice in the side of a cliff about 40 feet above the ground. Subsequent searches for the roost have been unsuccessful.

Because so little is known of the big free-tailed bat's basic biology and habitat requirements, surveys for summer and winter roosts are needed. Once a roost has been located and analyzed for potential threats, managers can develop protection and conservation recommendations. The biggest threat to this species, as with most other bats, is human disturbance at the roosts. This threat can be minimized though education, and by installing a locked gate at the entrance of the roost.

MERLIN D. TUTTLE PHOTOS

Family — *Molossidae*

Greater western mastiff bat

Eumops perotis californicus

The greater western mastiff bat is the largest bat in the United States, with a wingspan measuring more than 21 inches. Its ears protrude forward, giving the appearance of a "bonnet." This bat can be distinguished from other free-tailed and mastiff bats by its size alone. The average body length of this bat is 4 to 5 inches.

This bat is found in California, Nevada, Arizona, Texas, and Mexico. The population in Arizona is one of three widely separated populations; the other two being in South America and Cuba. It is resident in Arizona year-round. It lives in man-made and natural crevices, typically in upper Sonoran desertscrub.

Along with being the largest bat, the greater western mastiff is also the loudest bat in the United States. It emits a high pitched "cheap" every two to three seconds during flight. The call is distinctive and can be used to determine the bat's presence. These bats can also be identified by the sharp swishing sound made by their wings in flight. These sounds can be heard up to 100 feet away.

Since these bats are so large, flight from the ground is difficult. Their roost sites compensate for this difficulty by providing a large vertical drop. Most regularly used roosts are situated at cliffs over 20 feet in height, and have moderate to large openings that allow entry from below. These openings are approximately 2 inches wide, narrowing at the end to allow the bats to wedge in tightly. These bats are vocal in the roosts during the early morning and late afternoon, but emerge from the roost only after complete darkness.

Greater western mastiffs live in relatively small colonies, each generally of less than 100 individuals. The colonies can be recognized by massive urine stains and large guano droppings. The odor associated with them is stronger than for most other bats, due to an oil secretion from a throat gland. This gland seems to occur seasonally in males to attract females. Breeding occurs in the spring with generally one young born per female during the summer.

Because they are so large, these bats have a long foraging period, up to 6.5 hours each night. They usually forage 100 to 200 feet (sometimes up to 1,000 feet) above ground, and seldom use night roosts. They forage on various insects, especially bees, wasps, ants, and sawflies. Unlike most other bats, they do not seem to have activity peaks during the night.

The population trend and winter habits of this species are poorly known, but some roost sites are definitely no longer occupied. Identifying roost sites and foraging areas is crucial to proper management of this species. ▼

Family — *Molossidae*

MERLIN D. TUTTLE PHOTOS

Mexican free-tailed bat

Tadarida brasiliensis

The Mexican, Brazilian, or American free-tailed bat is a relatively small bat with brown fur and round ears. It belongs to a group of bats which has an extended tail beyond the tail membrane and long hairs on its feet. This species is one of the most widely distributed bats in the western hemisphere, thus the many common names. It occurs from northern South America and the Caribbean through the southwestern and southeastern United States. The average wingspread of this bat is 11.5 to 13 inches and the average body length is 2 to 2.5 inches.

Although most Mexican free-tailed bats migrate to and from Arizona, data suggests that some individuals overwinter and remain active at traditional Arizona roosts throughout the year. They roost primarily in caves, but also in mines, buildings, and bridges. This species forms great colonies, which may contain thousands to millions of individuals. The bats hang in clusters which blanket the roost walls and ceilings. The largest colony known in Arizona now contains an estimated 40,000 to 1 million bats during the spring and summer. Historically though, biologists estimated that as many as 20 million bats may have been present there.

Mexican free-tailed bats leave their roost at sundown and fly high and fast (up to 65 miles per hour) in search of their favorite food—moths—which they capture on the wing. As they exit the roost, their massive numbers appear as a black cloud which can be seen many miles away. They probably forage in groups at a feeding area which can be as far as 50 miles away from the roost.

Adults migrate to the southwestern United States during April, having already mated in February and March. The females assemble in maternity colonies to give birth and raise their young. Gestation takes 11 to 12 weeks; each female has one young, born in June or July. All the females in a colony give birth within a two-week period. During the day the young cling together in large masses separate from the adults. The mothers leave the young behind at night while they feed. The young develop rapidly and fly in about five weeks. The males and females reunite, usually in August, until October. Then they migrate south to warmer climates, where they remain active throughout the winter. During this biannual migration, they have been known to travel up to 800 miles.

Although the Mexican free-tailed bat population in Arizona seems stable (based on distribution rather than population counts), these bats are very susceptible to human disturbance, especially during the maternity season. Like many other bats, their low reproductive rate makes recuperation from a catastrophic disturbance difficult. Identification of maternity colonies is essential to protect and conserve this species. 🦇

Family — *Molossidae*

Pocketed free-tailed bat

Nyctinomops femorosaccus

The pocketed free-tailed bat is a medium-sized bat with a wingspread of 13 to 14 inches, a weight of 0.3 to 0.5 ounces, and an average body length of 2 to 3 inches. The fur is dark brown to gray. This species is distinguished by ears that are joined at the base, long narrow wings, and long foot hairs that protrude beyond the toes. The "pocket" for which this bat is named consists of a membrane that extends the length of the femur. The pocket is not readily noticeable, nor is it unique to this species as it occurs in other free-tailed bats.

The pocketed free-tailed bat ranges from southern California and New Mexico, south into Mexico through Baja, Sonora, Durango, and Jalisco at least to Michoacan. It is thought to be widespread in the Trans-Pecos region of Texas. It reaches the northern limits of its range in central Arizona. It seems to prefer caves and crevices along rocky cliffs in semi-arid desert lands. A large roost is known to exist under the roof tiles of the chemistry building at the University of Arizona.

Pocketed free-tailed bats live together in small colonies of less than one hundred individuals. Observation and collection suggest that this species does not migrate. Their roosts are sometimes disclosed by their loud and consistent, high-pitched squeaking. A single young is born during late June or early July.

These bats emerge from their roosts in groups of twos and threes, about 45 minutes after sunset. As they take to the air, they emit a loud high pitched call that sometimes continues during flight. They fly in a swift and unwavering manner as they search for insects on which to feed. They seem to find large moths most palatable. Pocketed free-tailed bats are able to drink while flying by forcefully striking the surface of a pond and scooping up a mouthful of water for an in flight refreshment.

Pocketed free-tailed bats occur frequently in southern Arizona, with central Arizona representing the northern boundary of their range. Though they are occasionally preyed upon by snakes, their biggest threat comes from humans. Limited knowledge of this species' natural history and habitat requirements has restricted management practices to locating roosts and protecting them from human disturbance. ❮

Underwood's mastiff bat
Eumops underwoodi

J. SCOTT ALTENBACH

Underwood's mastiff is a large bat, with a wingspan of 19 to 21 inches. Bats belonging to the family Molossidae, such as this one, are more commonly known as "free-tailed" bats, referring to their tail which extends beyond the tail membrane. The average body length of this bat is 4 to 4.5 inches.

The Underwood's mastiff bat has been studied extensively. Much of the available information has been collected from only a few localities. The known distribution of this species within Arizona and the United States is limited to the south-central part of the state, near the Baboquivari Mountains and the Organ Pipe National Monument. From there, its range extends south into the arid lowlands of Sonora and through the western

parts of Mexico into Honduras. It is presumed to be a year-round resident of Arizona, active primarily during the warm months, and hibernating high in rock crevices during the winter.

This mastiff bat tends to prefer Sonoran desertscrub and mesquite/grassland plant communities. It is commonly associated with species such as mesquite, willow, saguaro, ocotillo, cholla, and prickly pear. It appears to prefer roosting in crevices along steep cliffs, and possibly in the cracks of buildings. Its long, narrow wings provide poor maneuverability, thus requiring a vertical drop of as much as 30 to 40 feet from the roost site in order to launch into flight.

During the summer months, these bats drink water while in flight by gliding over water sources with large open surface areas, such as stock ponds. They may be detected by listening for their characteristic high-pitched "peeps," which are emitted several times per minute as they fly. These peeps are so intense they may actually hurt the observer's ears when the bat approaches too closely.

Although the reproductive process and food habits of the Underwood's mastiff bat are poorly understood, it is known that females give birth to a single young in late June or July. The primary diet of adults is night-flying insects.

Although much of the basic information required to properly manage this species is unknown, current management emphasis should be placed on protecting known roost and watering sites, which are limited.

Additional management needs include collection of basic information pertaining to its life history, habitat requirements, population status and trend, and distribution. As with many species whose northernmost range is in Arizona, management of this species is largely dependent upon cooperation with Mexico. ◥

Listening in the Dark ...
THE ART OF ECHOLOCATION

For every person who says "blind as a bat," another knows that "bats don't need to see, because they have radar." Neither perception is accurate, but something keeps bats from going bump in the night. That "something" is *echolocation*, and it is neither unique to bats (dolphins and shrews are also among the best known echolocators of the animal world) nor is it used by all bats (most of the flying-fox bats of the Old World depend upon their eyes for orientation).

Most bats communicate and navigate with high freqency sounds. Even in the dark, using sound alone they can detect obstacles as fine as human hair. When echolocating the bat's mouth is usually open, which explains the misconception we have developed regarding the bats apparent "attack" stance. Although the creature may appear fearsome when he is flying with his mouth open and teeth "bared" this is really just the navigation system at work.

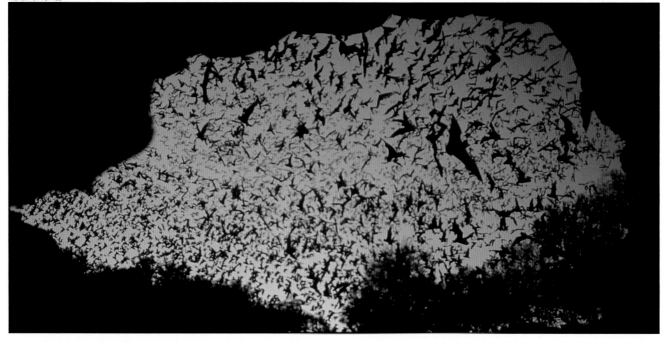

Animals that orient acoustically use sound waves to determine the position, size, shape, and even the texture of objects around them. In short, they use hearing the way most animals use vision. In echolocation, bats generally emit the orientation sounds themselves, and interpret the echos they receive. Stationary objects might represent potentially injurious obstacles to be avoided. Moving items might represent dinner to be captured.

Bats use both low and high frequency sounds to communicate. Low frequencies (mostly 4,000 to 20,000 Hz) can be detected by humans with normal hearing since the normal range of human hearing is 20 to 20,000 Hz. These sounds are typically used to communicate with other bats (as in mate recognition), when announcing a feeding territory, or in other social interaction. Low frequencies are also sometimes used to warn other bat traffic of a possible mid-air collision.

High frequency communication in bats occurs at levels beyond which the human ear can detect. Typically these "ultrasonic" sounds are in the 20,000 to 80,000 Hz range, but some bats emit at 120,000 to 210,000 Hz. The sound waves may be simple or complex. Each burst is usually short, measured in milliseconds, and may represent a single frequency or a narrow to very wide range of frequencies. Bursts may be pure tones, or have harmonics. The frequencies emitted are closely linked to the size of the bat's prey. Higher frequencies have shorter wavelengths, and are more useful in detecting smaller objects. Thus, in general, a small species of bat dependent on small prey would be expected to emit higher frequencies than would a big bat that typically feeds on larger prey.

Most bats produce their echolocation sounds from a larynx (voice box) that is much like that of any other mammal, but proportionately a bit larger. The sounds are emitted through the mouth in some species. Photographs of these bats in flight often show the open mouth, which some people misinterpret as an indication of ferociousness rather than recognizing it as related to echolocation. Thus starts fear, from the roots of misinformation.

In other species the sounds are emitted through the nose, and may be directed by a fleshy flap at the base of the nose. A similar flap at the base of the ear may affect sounds traveling toward the tympanum (eardrum). These flaps are not present in all bats, and their precise functions are not clearly known. Many other aspects of echolocation, other than simple mechanics, are also poorly understood. Form is often easier to understand than function.

How effective is echolocation in bats? Very effective, within a 1- to 9-foot radius. While in captivity, small bats have been detected capturing fruit flies in flight every three seconds, and when in the wild, every seven seconds. Some have detected—and avoided—wires thinner than a human hair. But perhaps the best measure of success is bat diversity. Since most species echolocate, and bats contribute roughly one-fourth of the world's species of mammals, their acoustic orientation must indeed be effective. And if you don't believe that, just sit outside on a summer night and listen in the dark yourself. These nocturnal aerialists are something to behold. ∨

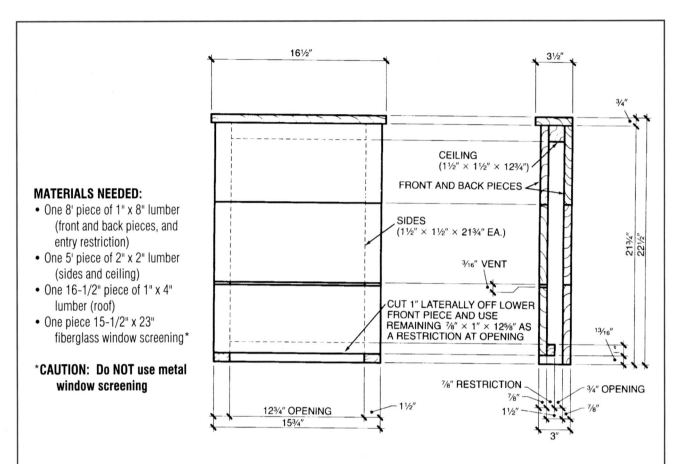

MATERIALS NEEDED:
- One 8' piece of 1" x 8" lumber (front and back pieces, and entry restriction)
- One 5' piece of 2" x 2" lumber (sides and ceiling)
- One 16-1/2" piece of 1" x 4" lumber (roof)
- One piece 15-1/2" x 23" fiberglass window screening*

*CAUTION: Do NOT use metal window screening

Diagram labels:
- 16½"
- 3½"
- ¾"
- CEILING (1½" × 1½" × 12¾")
- FRONT AND BACK PIECES
- SIDES (1½" × 1½" × 21¾" EA.)
- 3/16" VENT
- CUT 1" LATERALLY OFF LOWER FRONT PIECE AND USE REMAINING ⅞" × 1" × 12⅝" AS A RESTRICTION AT OPENING
- 21¾"
- 22½"
- 13/16"
- 12¾" OPENING
- 15¾"
- 1½"
- ⅞" RESTRICTION
- ¾" OPENING
- ⅞"
- ⅞"
- 1½"
- 3"

Beginner's Bat House

For years, people all over the world have constructed and installed nesting boxes for birds. In some cases, these artificial habitats have played a vital role in recovery of bird populations. Using this success as a model, Bat Conservation International (BCI) began popularizing bat houses in the early 1980s. Since then, thousands have been erected—some enormously successful, some not.

Recently, BCI evaluated the successes and failures of bat houses across the United States. Of the 276 bat houses included in the survey, 52 percent attracted bats. BCI also discovered that larger boxes with longer and taller roosting chambers were more successful than smaller houses with short roosting chambers. The most successful bat box design was tall and wide, with only one roosting chamber.

Admittedly, most of the information collected on these bat houses came from the mid-western and eastern United States. Because of Arizona's unique climate, additional factors such as heat and sun intensity must be taken into consideration. The new and improved bat house plans developed by BCI address these problems by adding insulation and additional roosting chambers.

Correct placement of the bat house is critically important to its success, especially in Arizona. The house should be placed in a very shady area, and high above the ground (20 to 30 feet for best results) to discourage predators. It could be placed on the north-facing wall of a house, carport or barn; high under the eves of a house or building; inside a carport, patio, or barn; or in a tree that provides shade for most of the day. If exposure to direct sunlight is unavoidable, the early morning sun would be more tolerable than the intense afternoon sun.

The most frequent inhabitants of southwestern bat houses are Mexican free-tailed bats. However,

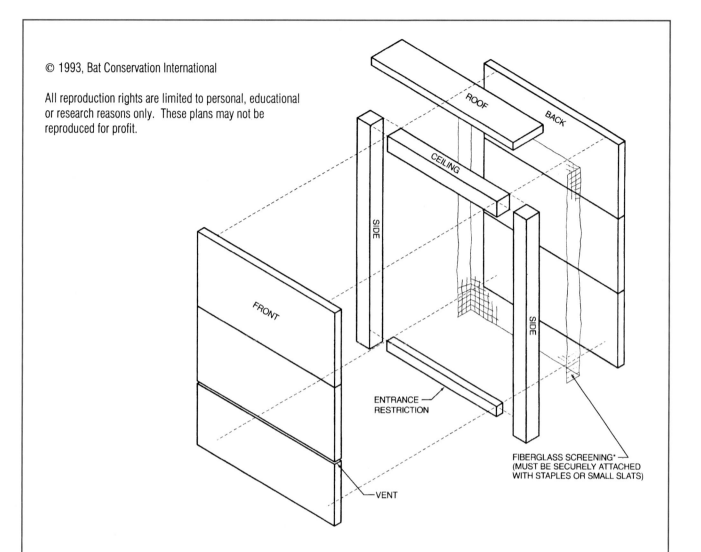

pallid bats immediately occupied a bat box in Prescott, Arizona after being excluded from their nearby attic roost. This quick possession was contrary to the long-held belief that it usually takes at least two years for a colony of bats to move in. The BCI survey also demonstrated that if a bat house is not occupied within the first two years, it will probably never be occupied. So, if you install a bat house and it does not attract a colony of bats within two years, move it!

Should you decide to install a bat house, monitoring its success is extremely important, but disturbing the colony could cause roost abandonment. One very effective way to monitor the house without disturbing the occupants is to observe it at dusk for emerging bats. If you suspect that a maternity colony is roosting in the bat house, quietly and quickly direct a red-filtered light into the box after dark and look for babies left behind while the female feeds. This should be done only once or twice during the summer; discontinue monitoring if the young become agitated. The house should also be monitored once or twice during the winter, as bats have been known to hibernate in bat houses in Texas, Kentucky, and New York. The Department is very interested in any data that you collect from your bat house. To report your success or failure, please write to: Nongame Branch, Arizona Game and Fish Department, 2221 W. Greenway Road, Phoenix, Arizona 85023.

For more information regarding bat houses, order a copy of "The Bat House Builder's Handbook" from BCI, at P.O. Box 162603, Austin, Texas 78716. ⋎

Herps of Arizona

HERPS

Arizona is home to more than 120 species of amphibians and reptiles, including about two dozen amphibians (frogs, toads and salamanders), a handful of turtles and one of the most diverse communities of snakes and lizards (more than 40 species apiece) to be found anywhere in the United States. Although this gives some Arizonans the willies, I'm happy they're here. After you become a little more familiar with these fascinating and often beautiful animals, I think you'll agree.

Like all other wildlife, amphibians and reptiles (for short we'll call them "herps," from a Latin word meaning "crawling") are important components of their natural ecosystems. Most herps prey on insects, arachnids, or small vertebrates and are in turn eaten by larger predators.

Anyone who has ever watched a Sonoran Desert toad eat insects under an outdoor light at night can attest to their prodigious appetite. Many farmers happily share their property with large gopher snakes that can consume an entire nest of small rodents in a few minutes. And desert tortoises, banded geckos, and Arizona treefrogs are just plain cute, in addition to filling important ecological roles.

In Arizona's desert ecosystems, herps often dominate other vertebrates in species diversity, numbers of individuals, and total biomass. Because of their basic biology, herps can more effectively exploit opportunities presented by the desert and they are less susceptible to its rigors. For starters, herps are ectotherms, which means they derive body heat from the external environment. Birds and mammals produce heat internally and are called endotherms. This single characteristic reduces basic energy needs of herps by about 90 to 95 percent compared to birds or mammals of similar body size. In the parched desert landscape, where plant productivity and energy availability are limited, energy efficiency gives herps a big edge on their endothermic counterparts.

As a group, herps are among the most feared and loathed of animals. Many of our beliefs are myths or misconceptions founded on ignorance. Their secretive nature makes most herps unfamiliar, and we tend to be dubious of the unknown. For example, how many birds do you see on your way to work, school or the grocery store? How many snakes?

In our effort to understand these animals better, Heritage funds and the Nongame Tax Checkoff have been invaluable. They have allowed the Department's Amphibians and Reptiles Program to continue ongoing projects and begin many new ones. They are the entire funding base for some studies and have been used to match dollars from other agencies and institutions for other projects.

We are working with such diverse cooperators as the Bureau of Land Management, the U.S. Fish & Wildlife Service, the U.S. Forest Service, the U.S. Bureau of Reclamation, the Las Vegas Valley Water District, the National Park Service and the University of Nevada, Las Vegas. These projects range from monitoring desert tortoise populations to deciphering taxonomic relationships of Arizona's leopard frogs. And we still have a lot of work to do if we are to meet our goals for conserving and learning from these fascinating, if often misunderstood and under-appreciated animals.

COLLARED LIZARD photo by George Andrejko

L·I·Z·A·R·D·S

lizards, of all the herps, are probably the most watchable. Arizona has at least 43 native species which is surpassed only by Texas. Most are active during the daytime and tend to be less shy than most other herps. Many of our common species are brightly colored, especially the males, and will carry out normal feeding and social behavior even with a human observer close by.

Have you ever seen a lizard on a rock or fencepost doing pushups or bobbing its head? This is usually a male, and he isn't doing calisthenics. These are social displays and their pattern, like bird songs, is unique to each species. Males perform these antics as territorial displays to other males or, in modified form, as courtship displays to females. In either case, the object is to demonstrate his size and vigor to other lizards.

Unlike the avoidance strategy that allows many of Arizona's amphibians to survive in desert habitats, most of Arizona's desert lizards have evolved mechanisms that allow activity during even the hottest and driest times of the year. In comparison to amphibians, and even birds and mammals, the skin of most desert lizards is nearly impervious to water.

Low reptilian metabolic rates allow low respiration rates, so lizards lose far less water through breathing than birds or mammals. Furthermore, reptiles excrete urine in solid form, as uric acid, the white powdery substance familiar from bird droppings. This requires far less water than the water soluble urea excretion of mammals or the ammonia excretion common to many amphibians. Finally, shelled amniotic eggs allow reproduction in the absence of the free standing water required by amphibians.

This combination of traits gives reptiles a big advantage in the invasion of arid habitats. In fact, lizards are among the most obvious diurnal desert animals throughout the warmer part of the year. On hot summer days, they may be active long after other vertebrates have retreated to cool shelters. During these times, lizards are exposed to few predators or competitors, except other lizards and perhaps a few snakes.

Even the most thermophilic (heat-loving) lizards face predators occasionally. An interesting array of anti-predation mechanisms has evolved, different lizards following different evolutionary pathways. For some, such as horned lizards (they aren't toads, by the way) and tree lizards (the little guys on wood or block fences in your backyard), the primary defense is cryptic coloration. When they sit still on a natural background they can be nearly impossible to see.

For some of the more visible species, such as bright green male collared lizards, large chuckwallas, or fast moving hyperactive whiptail lizards, speed and memorized escape routes may be more important means for staying alive.

When primary defenses fail, most North American lizards are able to shed their tails, leaving the predator with a wriggling but easily subdued meal. The lizard escapes with its life and regenerates its tail over the next several weeks.

One of the rarest and most interesting reproductive phenomena known among vertebrates is characteristic of at least five of Arizona's nine whiptail lizards. These species consist entirely of females that reproduce without mating. All offspring are females that are genetically identical to the mother. This form of clonal or asexual reproduction is known as parthenogenesis.

Asexual reproduction is common among plants and invertebrates but is unknown in birds and mammals. It has been observed in several lizards, three snakes, a few amphibians (some of the mole salamanders around the Great Lakes), and some fishes. 🦎

JEFF HOWLAND

BUNCH GRASS LIZARD

The bunch grass lizard is fairly common in its preferred habitat, the mountains and hills of southeastern Arizona, but it is not often seen. Its small size and cautious habits reveal its presence only to careful observers. When passing through the moderate to high elevation grassland and open woodland habitat of this lizard, look for a small, dark blur, darting from one bunch grass to another. After some patient pursuit, as the lizard sneaks through the maze of grasses around your feet, you might be rewarded with a good look at the boldly patterned, nervous little lizard. Bunch grass lizards feed on small insects and are in turn prey to ridgenose and twin-spotted rattlesnakes. 🦎

CHUCKWALLA

A large lizard, the chuckwalla sometimes exceeds 16 inches in total length. It is herbivorous, feeding on leaves, blossoms, and fruits of annual and perennial plants. It requires outcrops, boulders, and other rocky habitats, the more nooks and crannies the better. Chuckwallas emerge from hiding for feeding and socializing, usually in the early morning and late afternoon. After eating their fill, they retreat, remaining close to the surface, keeping their temperature high to aid digestion. When harassed, a

RICK BOWERS

chuckwalla wedges its flat body into a tight crevice and bloats itself with air. Granular scales on sandpaper-like skin grip the rock surface, making the lizard nearly immovable. Native Americans hunted chuckwallas, extracting them after deflating the distended body with a pointed stick. 🦎

CLARK'S SPINY LIZARD

The Clark's spiny lizard, one of the largest of the "blue-belly" lizards, grows to almost a foot in total length. A good way to distinguish this lizard from its close relative, the desert spiny lizard, is the presence of black bars on the forearms of the Clark's. This lizard's favorite perch, for basking and ambushing its prey, is often the trunk or a large branch of a

sycamore or cottonwood tree, but they also inhabit rock outcrops. They feed mostly on large insects, but may supplement their diet with flowers and an occasional leaf. You will probably hear this shy lizard scamper away into a rock crevice or high up into a tree more often than you will see it. 🦎

STEVE SMITH

STEVE SMITH

COLLARED LIZARD

To many people, the collared lizard appears rather dinosaur-like. Its seasonal predilection for fruits may belie that perception a bit, but when this ground-dwelling lizard gets up and running, the tyrannosaurus image comes clearly to mind. At top speeds, only its hind legs are used, weak forelegs folded limply along its sides and long tail extended backward to serve as a counterweight. Known as a sit-and-wait predator, the collared lizard is very patient. Perched atop a large rock or small boulder, it waits for a fat grasshopper, small lizard, or most anything else that is too small to eat it. With prey in sight, it springs into action, sometimes running down its meal after a chase of twenty yards or more.

DESERT IGUANA

As they clumsily climb through the branches of creosote bushes, eating bright yellow flowers as they go, desert iguanas watch for marauding leopard lizards. In mid-May, a female's ovarian follicles rapidly enlarge with yolk, the nutrient and energy supply for development of new desert iguanas. She mates when the eggs are ready for ovulation and then disappears underground. She will lay her eggs in some secret, carefully chosen spot beneath the parched desert flatland. She will not emerge again until late July, about a week before her young see sunlight for the first time. Does she nest in a side chamber of a kangaroo rat burrow? What does she do underground for ten weeks? Does she guard her incubating eggs from predators? Who knows?

RANDY BABB

DESERT SPINY LIZARD

The shy desert spiny lizard is common throughout Arizona, everywhere but the high elevation conifer forests of the central mountains. Because it is shy, it can be a little difficult to see. Watch for its form on a boulder or tree trunk at distances of 50 yards or more. By the time you get any closer, it moves to the far side of its perch (like a tree squirrel), disappears under a piece of bark, or dives into a crevice or pack rat nest. It has good reason to be wary. Its large size, for a lizard, draws the attention of airborne predators. Black hawks are a particular threat in riparian areas, while red-tailed hawks and roadrunners take over in the desert. 🦎

RICK BOWERS

GILA MONSTER

The gila monster is Arizona's only venomous lizard. The beaded body, fat tail, distinctive pattern and propensity for slow, deliberate movement make it very recognizable. Only the much-smaller banded gecko, which has a translucent belly and conspicuous vertical pupils (look carefully), is frequently mistaken for it. Most of the gila monster's time is spent in or, on warm winter days, lounging at the entrance to a den borrowed from or shared with a variety of other animals. But on warm spring days or summer nights, the gila monster meanders across the desert floor, in search of food. Constantly flicking its forked tongue as it goes, it samples the air for signs of prey, or predators. Like a mousetrap, when left alone it is perfectly harmless to humans. 🦎

CLAUDE STEELMAN

LESSER EARLESS LIZARD

Female lesser earless lizards often perch on small rocks, looming a few inches over the soil of their desert grassland home. They cock one eye at disturbances in the grass and raise the tail, waving it in the air. To a young whipsnake, the diversion is irresistible. It almost invariably grabs the tail, allowing the lizard to twist, detach its tail just above the snake's jaws, and dash under a rock. The snake struggles for a few seconds to subdue the thrashing tidbit and then, with the edge off its appetite, leaves in search of a larger meal. The lizard will forego production of a clutch of eggs, diverting surplus energy to tail regeneration. But she has learned a lesson and will reproduce later in the summer. 🦎

JEFF HOWLAND

R.A. WATSON

JEFF HOWLAND

LONG-NOSED LEOPARD LIZARD

As you might guess from its appearance, the long-nosed leopard lizard is closely related to the collared lizard, and runs very much like it but probably even faster. The leopard lizard is more a denizen of hot desert flatlands. Like the mammal from which it takes its name, the leopard lizard is a predator, a very good one. It roams through open desert creosote and bursage, seeking other lizards, for food rather than companionship. The leopard lizard's sharp, recurved teeth and powerful jaws are well adapted to holding onto what it catches. It may polish off incredibly large meals, sometimes nearly doubling its weight at a single sitting. A leopard lizard devouring an adult desert iguana, whole, is an amazing sight! (shown far left)

LONG-TAILED BRUSH LIZARD

Male long-tailed brush lizards bask in the early morning sun, hugging small twigs on the periphery of ironwood trees. A large male gladly shares his tree with several adult females and grudgingly tolerates one or two smaller adult males, as long as they stay away from him and the females. He ignores the dynamic pool of juveniles that come and go with the seasons. He decidedly does not ignore a large desert spiny lizard that emerges from a wood rat nest at the base of the tree, moving up onto the trunk and some of the larger branches. The spiny lizard is an effective predator and, when active, is a primary focus of attention for the brush lizards. (shown above)

MADREAN ALLIGATOR LIZARD

RANDY BABB

The Madrean alligator lizard is the only member of its family in Arizona. Most of its close relatives (other alligator lizards and galliwasps) have small, weak legs while others (glass lizards and slow worms) are entirely legless. When moving through tight spaces, Madrean alligator lizards often slither like snakes, with their hind legs folded against their sides. These slender lizards are typically associated with woodland habitats but may be found in grasslands and along higher desert riparian corridors. In summer, alligator lizards are active in late afternoon and early evening, foraging through wood piles, leaf litter, or other debris. Juvenile alligator lizards, like the one pictured, are strongly banded, while adults often sport more broken bands. Adult Madrean alligator lizards with unbroken tails may attain total lengths of a foot or more.

PLATEAU LIZARD

The plateau lizard of northern Arizona, a subspecies of the wide-ranging eastern fence lizard, lives at the western extreme of a geographical range that extends eastward to the Atlantic coast states, well south into Mexico and as far north as South Dakota. Its broad range and abundance have made it a favorite subject of scientific studies of geographic variation in everything from food preference to longevity. Do females from two areas with different climates produce different numbers of eggs during the course of a year? Are the differences attributable simply to food availability, or are they genetically determined? Elucidation of the environmental versus genetic bases of such characters provides the raw material biologists need to decipher the causal mechanisms behind evolutionary change. ✒

JEFF HOWLAND

SHORT-HORNED LIZARD

Most people think of "horny-toads" as desert animals, not denizens of pine country. Yet on a short afternoon walk on the Mogollon Rim you may see several, from five inch adults to quarter-sized juveniles, miniature replicas right down to their comical scowls. The geographic range of the short-horned lizard is the largest of all horned lizards. Extending northward from Mexico, it is the only horned lizard to reach Canada. Like several other lizards with northern or high elevation distributions, it is a live bearer. Why the correlation? Perhaps the mother is able to maintain a more favorable environment for developing embryos, by basking in moving patches of sunlight, than would be possible through even the most careful selection of a nest site for eggs. ✒

JEFF HOWLAND

SIDE-BLOTCHED LIZARD

Occurring from central Texas to the Pacific coast and in all of the major North American deserts, from western Washington to northern Zacatecas, Mexico, the side-blotched lizard is one of the most ubiquitous and abundant of our desert lizards. This is one of the few lizards that can be found active at nearly anytime of the year, even on sunny days in January. Breeding activity begins as early as February, making these the first lizards to lay eggs and the first hatchlings to appear in spring. During the hot summer months, side-blotches are the first lizards out in the morning. Activity begins just after sunrise and ceases by mid-morning, when most of the other lizards are at peak activity. ✒

RANDY BABB

TEXAS HORNED LIZARD

TROY CORMAN

One of six species of horned lizards in Arizona, the Texas horned lizard is found in desert grasslands in the extreme southeastern part of the state. Although its numbers have declined drastically in Texas and Oklahoma, our populations seem stable. Texas horned lizards have been found to squirt blood from the inner corner of the eye when attacked by canid predators (foxes or coyotes). The significance of this phenomenon is not clearly understood, but it is presumed to act as some sort of a deterrent to predation. Because they feed almost solely on ants, it has been hypothesized that horned lizard blood may contain foul-tasting or irritating chemicals, such as formic acid. Biologists studying this behavior in southeastern Arizona may soon have the answers.

TREE LIZARD

TROY CORMAN

The tree lizard is one of the few native herps that has successfully persisted in the urban Phoenix valley. Population densities of this small lizard may actually be higher now than they were before European settlers moved into the area. In their natural habitats, tree lizards live on trees, shrubs, boulders, and rock faces. Apparently, our wood and block fences and the sides of our houses are similar enough to these habitats for tree lizards to feel right at home. Because they face fewer of their natural predators in urban areas, and prey species such as crickets, cockroaches, and spiders are artificially abundant, their numbers have soared. Too bad most other herps haven't fared as well.

WESTERN BANDED GECKO

RANDY BABB

Banded geckos are common inhabitants of Arizona's deserts, from featureless creosote flats to rugged mountainsides. They spend the day in burrows of other animals or under surface debris. They are active at night, and one of only two nocturnal lizards native to the state. Geckos often wander into homes and garages, seeking shelter beneath boxes or other objects. When captured, they usually give a surprising squeak. Because of their banded color pattern, geckos are often mistaken for baby Gila monsters. In fact, a baby Gila monster, fresh out of the egg, is larger than the largest banded gecko and has a similar pattern but different colors. Unlike most lizards, banded geckos always lay two eggs at a time, about every month throughout the summer.

TROY CORMAN

WESTERN WHIPTAIL LIZARD

A typical day in the life of a western whiptail lizard begins with a little basking in the sun. After its body temperature reaches an acceptable level, it begins foraging. It concentrates its efforts on leaf litter, dead wood, and other flotsam that collects under trees and bushes. It turns over twigs, digs in loose dirt, and breaks open termite tunnels, feeding on the small invertebrate treasures it uncovers. It flicks its tongue constantly, looking for clues as to the whereabouts of hidden prey. It may sit still and listen for the digging sounds of subterranean beetle grubs or scorpions, which it excavates and consumes. Like an angler at a good fishing hole, it spends more time under productive bushes and less under those whose rewards are more sparing. 🦨

M.L. ANDERSON

ZEBRA-TAILED LIZARD

With nose pointed toward the sun, tail and toes elevated, and legs stretched, raising its body above blistering desert pavement, a zebra-tailed lizard surveys its territory on a hot July morning. Occasionally it shuttles between sun and shade, keeping its body temperature balanced at a comfortable 106 degrees F. It watches for three things: prey, predators, and other zebra-tailed lizards. Little else is of any real interest. It pounces on a small bee visiting a nearby flower. When threatened by a coachwhip snake, it darts to the nearest shelter, running along a memorized escape route with its black and white tail raised and waving. Encroaching male zebra-tailed lizards are dealt with harshly while females are greeted with ardent courtship displays. This is living! 🦨

T·U·R·T·L·E·S

urtles and tortoises are probably the oldest of the surviving herp lineages. Fossil forms first appeared in the Triassic period, near the beginning of the long reign of dinosaurs. The arid Southwest is isolated from the diverse freshwater turtle fauna of the eastern United States by the continental divide. As a result, we have only four or five native species of turtles and two of these are terrestrial.

The only two aquatic species that are known with some degree of certainty to be native are two species of mud turtles. They are substantially more tolerant of occasional desiccation than are most aquatic turtles of eastern North America. This tolerance may have been the key factor in their successful invasion.

The most obvious characteristic common to all turtles is the protective shell. The ribs and vertebral column are fused to bony plates that effectively surround the vulnerable body. Most are able to withdraw the head, legs, and tail into the shell leaving only a small fraction of their body exposed.

For young turtles, whose shells are soft and pliable, the world is a dangerous place. If they can grow and survive their first few years, the shell hardens and becomes an effective barrier to many predators.

Turtles are further characterized by long life spans (some exceeding 100 years) and an overall conservative and patient approach to life. Unlike most long-lived animals, turtles tend to produce large numbers of relatively small eggs, partially a consequence of physical limitations imposed by the bulky shell. These small eggs result in small young that are susceptible to a variety of perils not faced by the adults. This, like their legendary slowness, is the price turtles pay for their armor.

Diets of turtles range from completely carnivorous to herbivorous. Turtles are well known for their ability to store fat. Depending on the species, a large adult may be able to survive two years of drought without feeding, and females may even be able to lay eggs during this time.

When food becomes available again, they may eat enough in a few weeks to provide all the energy necessary to recover from their period of starvation and last long into the future. Larger species generally are able to store proportionally more fat and survive longer without food, with less hardship, than smaller species.

Perhaps the best example of this ability among Arizona turtles is provided by the desert tortoise. When necessary, adults may spend the greater part of two years or more, deep in a shelter or burrow. They also make use of these shelters during the hottest and driest portions of normal years. On many occasions, while reaching for a desert tortoise in its sheltersite, I have envied the 80 degree temperatures that I could feel with my fingertips while the rest of my body was exposed to 100+ degrees!

A wide variety of lizards, snakes, spiders, insects, and other inquilines often share the tortoise's comfortable domicile. This makes it a particularly important provider for many of the animals in its ecosystem. 🐢

DESERT BOX TURTLE

Desert box turtles are usually seen as they try, often unsuccessfully, to cross roads through the plains and semi-desert grasslands they occupy in southeastern Arizona. Slow moving, these turtles are no match for a speeding car. Away from the highway, adult box turtles spend much of their time in burrows, or rambling about in search of almost anything edible. Fruits and vegetables are among their staples, but so are all kinds of invertebrates. They may also reap a caloric reward for stumbling onto a nest of hairless baby mice. This turtle is aptly named for its shell. With head and legs withdrawn into the shell, the hinged lower half is pulled firmly up against the top half, leaving would-be predators no access to vulnerable soft body parts.

TROY CORMAN

DESERT TORTOISE

Like a natural ATV, but one with a strong and innate respect for the integrity of its desert home, the desert tortoise traverses some of the most rugged and least hospitable terrain in the Sonoran Desert. It is well built for its existence: hard shell, retractable head, and skin too tough even for cholla to penetrate. Excellent burrowers, equipped with muscular forelimbs and heavy claws, they dig shelters up to 15 feet deep. Desert tortoises may live up to 100 years, often remaining in an area of only a few square miles for their entire life and using the same shelter, on and off, for decades at a time. In severe droughts, females may forego reproduction, waiting for a year with good rainfall. Survival of young depends on productive plant growth.

GEORGE ANDREJKO

SONORAN MUD TURTLE

Sonoran mud turtles give off an odor when handled, a characteristic earning such uncomplimentary names as "stinkpot" and "musk turtle" for related species. Sonoran mud turtles are almost always found in or adjacent to water, including springs, streams, rivers, ponds, lakes, and rock pools of Arizona's deserts. When disturbed, they swim to the floor of the pool and bury themselves, slip under a rock, or simply lay still on a stony bottom, relying on their algae-covered shell to blend in. Sex of mud turtles, like most turtles, is determined by incubation temperature of the eggs. Nests at extreme temperatures (those in open sun or deep shade) produce almost all female young, while those at intermediate temperatures produce mostly males. An easy way to pick the sex of your offspring!

HOWARD LAWLER

GEORGE ANDREJKO

SPINY SOFTSHELL

The strange spiny softshell turtle, with its small head, pancake shaped body, and paddle-like rear limbs, looks like a frisbee with feet. Although introduced, it is well established in all of Arizona's major river systems and many lakes. Softshells often burrow into sand or mud in shallow water, seeming to disappear. The long neck extends to the surface where the pointed nose acts as a snorkel. In this way, they wait to ambush fish for hours at a time. Eggs are laid in spring and hatch in about 90 days. Unlike most turtles, the sex of spiny softshells is determined genetically. Spiny softshells are legal to take for food but beware—in rivers other than the Colorado they contain high levels of pesticides and consumption is not advisable.

WESTERN PAINTED TURTLE

CATHY ILLG

The painted turtle, an abundant freshwater turtle of the eastern and northern United States, occurs at only a few localities in Arizona. It's probably not native to any of them. These turtles bask in large numbers on logs, rocks, and even each other. The first sign of an intruder stimulates a mass bailout, turtles diving in every direction, often swimming directly to the safety of the muddy bottom or a hole in the bank. Males have long claws on their front feet, which they vibrate under the chin of the larger female during courtship. This apparently titillates, putting her in a more receptive mood. She lays eggs in summer, they hatch in fall, and the young remain in the nest until the first warm days of spring.

GREEN TOAD *photo by Randy Babb*

A·M·P·H·I·B·I·A·N·S

mphibians include frogs and salamanders. The name "toad" is commonly used for frogs that have a short, squat body form. On a global scale, there are over 4,000 species of frogs and toads and about 4,500 amphibians. At about 24 natives and four exotics, our amphibian diversity is modest.

Although larval forms of some species eat plants and others eat animal prey, adults of all living amphibians are carnivores. Most frogs use two criteria to decide whether an object qualifies as food: Does it move? Can I fit it in my mouth? Sometimes they even make exceptions to these. Our studies of bullfrog diets have turned up everything from large rocks and sticks to such unpalatable items as giant water bugs and tarantula wasps to rare Mexican garter snakes and endangered gila topminnows.

Aquatic frogs, such as leopard frogs and bullfrogs, are renowned for their ability to leap to a cover site in the water or surrounding vegetation. Their shyness and athletic talents are among their primary defenses against predators. The more modestly muscled true toads and spadefoots rely on foul tasting and toxic skin secretions. Glands in the skin produce these toxins, which ooze to the surface when the toad is accosted.

Though death is uncommon, the effects can be fairly drastic, including hallucinations, convulsions, and prolonged unconsciousness. Rubbing your eyes after handling a toad may result in a strong burning sensation, so wash your hands! Contrary to old beliefs, a toad's "warts" are not contagious.

Adult amphibians are characterized by glandular skin that is fairly permeable to water, so they lose water quickly by evaporation when exposed to hot or dry conditions. All but one of Arizona's amphibians have an aquatic larval stage in their life cycle. Strangely enough, most of our amphibians are found in desert or semi-desert habitats.

Their success has been allowed by the evolution of life histories and behavioral strategies that avoid situations where water loss is intolerably high. Some, such as the lowland leopard frog and canyon treefrog, are restricted to streams, springs, and other small areas with permanent water. Most of the others simply limit their

activity to times of the year when water is available.

Nearly all of our true toads and spadefoot toads spend the majority of their lives underground. They may be as far as three feet below the surface, where conditions remain cool and moist even at the hottest and driest times of the year. They are completely inactive, with their metabolism slowed to a state nearly indistinguishable from death. The heart may beat only once in a few minutes and breathing ceases almost entirely. This results in tremendous energy conservation and very little loss of water. What are they waiting for? The summer rains.

From their subterranean resting places, these frogs can detect vibrations caused by raindrops striking the ground. A sufficiently long and hard rain stimulates them to make their way back up to the surface. After the first heavy monsoon storms, these frogs emerge in huge numbers and flock to temporary ponds and puddles.

Males begin calling almost immediately and breeding activity begins within a day or two after females arrive. Tadpoles may hatch within 24 hours and begin feeding on algae and other microorganisms. Some species metamorphose into tiny toads within three weeks. Many temporary breeding ponds will dry before the tadpoles complete their development unless subsequent rains replenish the water supply.

Both young and adults remain active, mostly at night, throughout the summer rainy season. They feed gluttonously on insects, which are abundant during the monsoons, building their fat reserves for the long period of dormancy to follow. When autumn approaches, they burrow into the ground, backfilling their way as they descend. If the summer rains fail, the toads just wait. Sometimes two or even three years may pass before adequate rains elicit activity. 🐸

ARIZONA TOAD

Human alteration of wildlife habitat often has unforeseen results. Twentieth century modification of riparian areas is threatening, among dozens of other species, the Arizona toad. Arizona toads breed in flowing water. Closely related Woodhouse's toads breed in standing water. Damming, water diversion, groundwater pumping, and other disruptive water-use practices have converted flowing rivers and streams to ponds, lakes, or dry riverbeds. Some of the Arizona toad's former breeding habitat is now dry, while much of the remainder is suitable only for Woodhouse's toads. Many of the remaining populations of Arizona toads are small and surrounded by larger populations of Woodhouse's toads that may replace them through competition or hybridization. Fortunately, the situation is not yet desperate and efforts to preserve remaining riparian areas should save the Arizona toad. 🐾

JEFF HOWLAND

ARIZONA TREEFROG

In June, with the onset of the monsoon, Arizona treefrogs head to temporary marshes, ponds, and small lakes for a brief, explosive annual event: breeding. The lack of fish in these intermittent waters reduces competition and predation pressure for treefrog tadpoles. In many of the fishless lakes of Arizona, tiger salamander larvae are the top carnivores; the treefrog tadpoles are herbivorous, and sometimes occur in the same ponds. When they do, they are eaten by the growing salamanders. Sometimes these lakes teem with salamanders and the frogs shift their breeding activity to nearby rain pools, free of waterdogs. These smaller pools often dry before the tadpoles complete development and metamorphose into frogs. Maybe it's better to risk desiccation than to taunt a tiger salamander. 🐾

RANDY BABB

RANDY BABB

BARKING FROG

The barking frog is a member of the largest genus of frogs in the entire world, with over 400 described species. Only a handful of barking frogs have been collected in Arizona. They breed after the first substantial summer thunderstorms. Otherwise, life history is poorly known, but we can make inferences from knowledge of related species. The male probably guides an interested female to a pre-selected nest site, deep in a cool, damp rock crevice. If she approves, eggs are laid and fertilized and she leaves him in charge. He guards them from small predators, keeps them from drying, and prevents invading fungi from damaging the developing embryos. The young frogs pass through the tadpole stage inside the egg and hatch as tiny barking froglets in about a month. 🐾

GEORGE ANDREJKO

BULLFROG

Bullfrogs are abundant in permanent waters across most of Arizona. They have made themselves at home here, and in many other western states, since being introduced several decades ago by people who thought they would provide a good source of food. In fact, frog legs are a delicious and much under-utilized resource. Unfortunately, bullfrogs have become a real problem for many native species of amphibians, reptiles, and fishes, which they consume ravenously at every opportunity. Though not the sole cause, we suspect they have played a role in declines of Mexican garter snakes, several species of leopard frogs, and some of our threatened and endangered fishes. Do Arizona's threatened native wildlife a favor: buy a fishing license and harvest some bullfrogs! 🐾

TROY CORMAN

CANYON TREEFROG

Hiking a steep-walled canyon at dusk on a warm spring day, you hear a clattering sound, almost obscured by water tumbling over rocks—a herd of sheep? Maybe it's a breeding chorus of canyon treefrogs. They are well-adapted to canyon dwelling in the arid southwest. Their expanded, sticky toe tips enable them to scale steep canyon walls. Their skin is granular and resists water loss. The degree of color matching between skin and local rocks is sometimes uncanny. When walking through a canyon, watch carefully, the little stone that seems to jump out from under your foot may deserve a closer look. Or you may be fortunate enough to find a group of canyon treefrogs lined up single file in a fissure on a granite boulder. 🐾

CHIRICAHUA LEOPARD FROG

Until recently, leopard frogs across the country were classified as a single species, long established regional differences in appearance being dismissed as simple geographic variation. In the 1960s, biologists realized that, among other things, these "geographic variants" rarely interbred, even when found in the same pond. This reproductive isolation, at that time one of the main criteria used in defining different species, led herpetologists to suspect there are a dozen or more species of leopard frogs in the United States. Nearly half of them are native to Arizona. The Chiricahua leopard frog is one of the most recently recognized, having been described in 1979. This is our most highly aquatic species, living in mountain streams and ponds from 3500 to 8500 feet in central and southeastern Arizona. 🐾

JEFF HOWLAND

SONORAN DESERT TOAD

Largest of our native amphibians, the Sonoran Desert toad may sometimes tip the scales well in excess of two pounds. Sometimes seen in late spring, the main stimulus of activity is the summer rains. Toxic, hallucinogenic skin secretions are this toad's main defense against predators, making it quite unpopular with pet owners in our desert regions. These large toads are still fairly common on the outskirts of large urban areas and interactions with humans are therefore frequent. Unfortunately, many people react negatively to their presence and the Department receives numerous requests for information on how to rid them from residential areas. If we eliminated them from residential areas, how many more millions of crickets and cockroaches would we have to deal with? 🐾

BRUCE TAUBERT

COUCH'S SPADEFOOT

The croaking call of the Couch's spadefoot is familiar throughout southern Arizona's deserts, even in moderately developed areas around Phoenix and Tucson. The males are among the first frogs to congregate at temporary pools and begin calling after summer thunderstorms, attempting to attract gravid females. They may gather at almost any standing water, even puddles in a road. Within a few days, eggs are laid and tadpoles emerge. Feeding on abundant microorganisms in the ponds, tadpoles grow and develop rapidly, transforming into small spadefoots in as little as three weeks. Unless water lost to evaporation or percolation into the soil is replenished by subsequent rains, smaller ponds may dry, returning nutrients from the tadpoles to the mud, from whence they are recycled the next time the pond fills. 🐾

TROY CORMAN

TROY CORMAN

GREAT PLAINS TOAD

Raucous choruses of Great Plains toads are familiar across most low elevation areas of Arizona. The combination of large numbers of toads, a loud and long call, and a tendency to breed for several nights after large rains has led some people to find these toads offensive. Post-breeding dispersal from ponds leads to direct encounters, some toads even having the audacity to burrow under our fences to gain entrance to our back yards. They have been blamed for insomnia, clogging swimming pool filters, and a host of other problems. In reality, though, isn't it we who have invaded their back yard? It is easy to observe Great Plains toads during breeding choruses. Get to know them and maybe you'll actually enjoy hearing them sing a few times each year. ✎

JEFF HOWLAND

LOWLAND LEOPARD FROG

Different species of leopard frogs look so much alike, how do they tell each other apart for breeding? Each species has a unique male advertisement call that functions to attract mates or ward off competing males. Between species, calls differ in duration, pitch, and other characteristics. In species that breed for extended periods of time, like leopard frogs, females select a mate from among calling males. They may use call characteristics, like loudness or rate of repetition, to help them pick. Presumably, these characteristics indicate size or health of the male, and therefore genetic quality. Alternatively, they may mate with the male who controls the best territory for egg laying. Either way, they are attempting to ensure that their offspring are sired by a male with good genes. ✎

NORTHERN CASQUE-HEADED FROG

The small northern casque-headed frog reaches the northern limits of its geographical distribution in south-central Arizona. Here it inhabits mesquite grasslands, but may be found in both thorn forest and thorn scrub in Mexico. The majority of this frog's life is spent entombed beneath the earth's surface within a parchment-like "cocoon." This structure is made of many layers of molted skin and prevents dehydration during the long months of inactivity. When summer rains fill low areas with water, these frogs quickly gather to breed. The males establish calling sites along the water's edge and solicit the attention of the females with a cowbell-like call. During the remainder of the summer wet season, casque-headed frogs spend their time fattening themselves for their long inactive periods. ❦

CECIL SCHWALBE

PACIFIC TREEFROG

Camouflaged Pacific treefrogs call during winter and spring, and are difficult to find away from a breeding pond. Usually marbled brown or green, skin color changes depending on a variety of environmental factors, often matching the frog's surroundings. Their toes have pads which allow them to climb vertically up a pane of glass or up into vegetation, where they may croak at the sign of approaching rain. Sporadically introduced to Arizona from the Pacific Coast states, usually in imported plants, these frogs have become well established in portions of the Colorado River Valley. While walking beside water near the Arizona/California border, don't be surprised to find an emerald green Pacific treefrog hiding in the grass. ❦

RANDY BABB

MARTY CORDANO

RAMSEY CANYON LEOPARD FROG

Imagine discovering a new frog species. In the rain forest, right? No, here in Arizona! That's what Dr. Jim Platz did. A leopard frog, known only from Ramsey Canyon and a few adjacent drainages in the Huachuca Mountains, is our state's most recently recognized amphibian. Why did dozens of naturalists dismiss these populations as Chiricahua leopard frogs? No one ever looked closely enough. When Dr. Platz did, he discovered something remarkably different. Curious that he had never heard them call, he stuck a microphone into the water one night and bingo! They call underwater! 🐸

GEORGE ANDREJKO

RED-SPOTTED TOAD

Red-spotted toads are named for their red warts. Though red-spotted toads may be found in grasslands and creosote flats, they are more often associated with rocky areas in paloverde-saguaro habitats. These toads are excellent climbers, as toads go, and often shelter in rock crevices. The male's advertisement call is a musical trill. The call can be heard on warm nights even in winter, but breeding usually occurs after spring or summer rains. Red-spotted toads are often found at isolated oases in dry desert mountain ranges. At sites that dry periodically or that are isolated from other permanent aquatic sites, this is often the only amphibian present. As long as there's water, red-spotted toads remain active. When it dries, they go dormant. 🐸

GEORGE ANDREJKO

SONORAN GREEN TOAD

The Sonoran green toad ranges into south-central Arizona from northern Sonora, Mexico. These small, beautiful toads breed in temporary ponds during and after monsoon rains, with males enthusiastically giving their wheezy, buzzer-like call. The remainder of the year is spent in subterranean burrows in brumation, a state of greatly reduced metabolism and no activity. Sonoran green toads feed on smaller invertebrates than other toads of comparable size. One favorite food item is winged termites, which emerge from their nests in tremendous numbers after summer rains but are available as food for only a few nights each year. The life history of the Sonoran green toad takes advantage of ephemeral water and food resources while avoiding the lean times of winter cold and early summer heat and drought. 🐸

SOUTHERN SPADEFOOT

For a southern spadefoot toad, being the "early bird" at a breeding pond may have tremendous benefits for the success of its offspring. The largest tadpoles, usually hatched from the first eggs laid, may become cannibalistic. They develop large heads, muscular jaws, and a strong carnivorous beak. Cannibals consume other tadpoles and invertebrates and grow more rapidly than non-cannibals. They metamorphose sooner, before the pond dries, and at a larger size, are better prepared for life on land. Cannibalism could probably not have evolved without the pre-existing ability of tadpoles to recognize siblings. Natural selection then favored individuals that fed only on non-siblings, allowing the genes that cause cannibalism to become widespread in spadefoot populations rather than eating themselves into oblivion. 🐾

JEFF HOWLAND

TARAHUMARA FROG

The Tarahumara frog is the only native amphibian known to have been eliminated from Arizona. Never widespread, they were common at a few isolated sites in south-central Arizona as recently as the late 1970s. Around 1978, frogs from the two largest known populations began to die. By 1983 they were gone. The cause is unknown to this day. It's believed acid precipitation and particulate fallout from smelters and other industries may have resulted in toxic levels of certain heavy metals in the mountain canyons and plunge pools where these frogs once thrived. This is just one of several frogs in the western U.S. and dozens in the world that have suffered large-scale declines in the past 20 years. Maybe we should heed the warning signs and clean up our act! 🐾

RANDY BABB

WESTERN CHORUS FROG

Water droplets from a snow drift quietly feed a growing pond. February on the Mogollon Rim produces chilly morning temperatures, but male western chorus frogs seem oblivious. Sporadic choruses of their methodical "prreeps" continue through the day and into early evening. Chorus frogs breed in spring, starting before the winter snows melt. Their eggs, deposited in late February, produce a pulse of dime-sized metamorphs in June. Through summer, juveniles run a gauntlet between the jaws of birds and garter snakes, growing to adult size before winter. In Arizona, chorus frogs are found in pinyon-juniper and ponderosa pine country. Though members of the treefrog family, they are not much for climbing. They prefer small cavities under logs and rocks, rarely venturing any distance from their breeding ponds.

JEFF HOWLAND

WOODHOUSE'S TOAD

Woodhouse's toads are common from the deciduous forests of the Atlantic coast to the deserts of southern California. They have persisted well in the face of extensive habitat alteration by humans. In the western states, reservoirs, irrigation, and urban ponds have actually expanded the amount of suitable habitat. Woodhouse's toads are prolific breeders, concentrating their reproductive efforts in the spring months. Males call in large choruses, sounding rather like distressed sheep. A single female can lay tens of thousands of eggs at one time. The bottoms of breeding ponds may be blanketed with minuscule black tadpoles. When they begin to metamorphose in late spring, each step around a breeding pond must be made carefully to avoid the tiny toads that hop out from underfoot.

WESTERN RATTLESNAKE *photo by R. A. Watson*

S·N·A·K·E·S

Species of snakes total nearly 2,700 planetwide. Only about 50 of them are found in Arizona. Less than one fourth of our species are venomous. Even so, with 11 rattlesnakes and one coral snake, Arizona leads the nation in total number of species of venomous snakes.

All snakes are carnivorous, and in Arizona their prey range from termites to jackrabbits. Some are very picky about what they eat. The Sonoran coral snake feeds almost exclusively on small snakes, occasionally taking smooth scaled lizards. Others, such as the California kingsnake, have broader tastes, eating birds, rodents, lizards, and other snakes (even rattlesnakes) with equal relish.

Probably the most striking characteristic of snakes is their lack of legs. Loss of limbs was presumably an adaptation that accompanied a shift toward a more fossorial (underground) existence by the legged ancestors of snakes. They are highly efficient at negotiating tight spaces.

Although some snakes have retained the underground lifestyle, others have become aquatic, arboreal, or terrestrial. Species having each preference are represented in Arizona. Snakes are actually descended, relatively recently, from the same extinct group of lizards that gave rise to gila monsters and the giant monitor lizards.

Although most people think of snakes as a lowly life form, they are actually highly advanced and extremely successful from an evolutionary perspective. The venom delivery apparatus and heat sensing pits of rattlesnakes are two examples of highly specialized adaptations.

Most of our snakes, like the lizards and frogs, occur in desert habitats. Their strategies for survival tend to be somewhat intermediate between these other two groups. Like their close relatives, the lizards, they have low rates of water loss because of their relatively waterproof skin and uric acid secretion.

Like our desert frogs, they tend to be active at night when temperatures are lower and relative humidity is higher. This coincides with peak activity of the prey of most of the larger snakes. Also like some frogs, garter snakes are almost completely restricted to sites that have permanent water. This is closely related to their diet of fish, waterdogs, frogs, and tadpoles.

If we can look past our deeply ingrained prejudices against snakes, we see some very beautiful animals with fascinating biology. The delicate brown vine snake, the tiny and seldom encountered shovel-nosed snake, and even the western diamondback all have interesting stories.

From most snakes, we have nothing to fear. Even those that are capable of harming a human will usually take advantage of any opportunity to escape without biting. About half of all reported venomous snakebites in Arizona are suffered by people who are intentionally interacting with the snake. When treated with the caution and respect they deserve, there is little need to fear our venomous snakes.

BANDED ROCK RATTLESNAKE

The "Mexican" mountains of southeastern Arizona are famous for three small species of rattlesnakes, the banded rock, ridgenose, and twin-spotted. The two-foot banded rock is the most widely distributed and the most frequently encountered. It is found on rock ledges and along rocky hillsides above 5,000 feet elevation. The high-pitched buzz of its rattle has thrilled many a hiker bush-whacking up a steep slope. Banded rocks prey on lizards and small mammals, and are especially conspicuous when sunning immediately after brief summer showers. In new-born banded rock rattlers, as in many juvenile pit vipers, the end of the tail is bright yellow. Many of these species twitch the bright tail, like a fishing lure, to attract small prey. 〰

BLACK-TAILED RATTLESNAKE

The most widely distributed of Arizona's 11 species of rattlesnakes is the black-tail, or, as some people know it, the velvet-tail. It is a medium to fairly large-sized rattlesnake. It occurs from southeastern Arizona (across the central mountains and desert canyons) to the Grand Canyon above Lake Mead, although in many parts of its range it is quite local. The black-tail is a very handsome snake; in some individuals the light markings above may be almost golden, or bronze. Others have a greenish cast. Were it not for its delightful habit of "standing up" on muscular coils as it announces its presence, the black-tail would likely often be overlooked by hikers because its colors blend in so well with its surroundings. 〰

BROWN VINE SNAKE

Just how skinny is a brown vine snake? Well, at the typical Arizona length of about four feet, from tip of nose to tip of tail, it would take about 30 adults to equal the weight of a single diamondback rattlesnake of equal length! Small wonder the vine snake scarcely bends a twig as it winds its way through the branches of shrubs and trees, searching for lizards, insects, and small birds or mammals. Once captured, the prey is immobilized by the potent venom of this rear-fanged snake. Even for humans a bite can be painful, though no fatalities have been re-corded. Next time you go swinging through grapevines in a south-central Arizona canyon along the Mexican border, be careful. 〰

JEFF HOWLAND

RANDY BABB

TROY CORMAN

ROBERT CAMPBELL

CALIFORNIA KINGSNAKE

The California kingsnake, a subspecies of the common kingsnake, is an inhabitant of middle and lower elevations. It is at home in desert riparian and agricultural areas and up into chaparral. This species, in one or another of its numerous forms (subspecies), occurs from coast to coast across North America. Perhaps one reason for the common kingsnake's broad geographic range is its varied diet of other vertebrates, including snakes, lizards, birds, small mammals, and amphibians. Like many non-venomous snakes, kingsnakes are powerful constrictors. Prey capture begins with a lightning strike. In a quick, fluid motion, the snake wraps itself around the prey and then tightens its coils a little bit each time the animal exhales. This eventually leads to suffocation rather than crushing, as is often believed. ᗉᗉ

MARTY CORDANO

CHECKERED GARTER SNAKE

Relative to other garter snakes in Arizona, the slightly more terrestrial habits of checkered garter snakes may have spared them the high mortality rates suffered by narrow-headed and Mexican garter snakes at the hands (or mouths) of introduced predatory fishes and bullfrogs. Checkered garter snakes actually seem to be increasing their geographic range in Arizona, perhaps moving into ponds and streams vacated by declining populations of the more aquatic garter snakes. Irrigation ditches have been another boon to this species, one of the few herps which can be found in agricultural areas. Here they feed on some of the few other species, such as Woodhouse's toads, that are also able to tolerate the pesticides, herbicides, and other foreign aspects of these artificial habitats. ᗉᗉ

DESERT KINGSNAKE

The desert kingsnake is a subspecies of the common kingsnake. It intergrades (hybridizes) freely with the black kingsnake and the California kingsnake at the western extreme of its range. This clearly demonstrates that they are all members of the same species. Desert kingsnakes have broad tastes and prey on most any animal they can subdue, including rattlesnakes. If bitten, they have blood proteins that counteract the effects of the venom. During the hot summer, the desert kingsnake is nocturnal, seeking shelter from the heat in burrows or beneath surface objects. Activity of these snakes increases with the onset of the monsoons and they are sometimes encountered on remarkably cool summer nights. ᗉᗉ

JEFF HOWLAND

GOPHER SNAKE

The gopher snake can be found almost anywhere in Arizona. People often confuse other snakes, from whipsnakes to garter snakes, for this species. Likewise, their size and coloration lead many to confuse harmless gopher snakes with rattlesnakes. A tendency to hiss and vibrate the tail when confronted by a perceived enemy may further cloud the observer's ability to properly identify a gopher snake. This confusion may be beneficial to the gopher snake when the confusee is a predator, but it often has drastic consequences when a human is involved. Gopher snakes catch small mammals, birds and lizards, and like boas, they constrict their prey. Interestingly, this is probably the largest snake in Arizona, some exceeding seven feet in total length! ᐯᐯ

ROBERT CAMPBELL

GREEN RAT SNAKE

One of several tropical reptiles to reach the northern limits of its geographical range in southern Arizona, the green rat snake is the only rat snake in the state. Little is known about this elusive animal's ecology. It is known to inhabit several mountain ranges near the Mexican border and is often found in canyons with thick vegetation. Apparently green rat snakes feed on a wide variety of smaller vertebrates: birds, rodents, and lizards are all thought to be included on their menu. Like most rat snakes, green rat snakes are good climbers. Juveniles are not green at all, but distinctly patterned with brown blotches on a light background. As they mature, they assume the unicolored green of adulthood. ᐯᐯ

MARTY CORDANO

CECIL SCHWALBE

RICK BOWERS

GROUND SNAKE

"There's a snake in my house," blurts the voice on the other end of the phone. After some questioning about size and coloration, it is usually determined that the snake is a ground snake. Ground snakes are one of only a few species that do pretty well in the face of human development and are often found in and around urbanized areas. In the Department's Phoenix office, most of the snake calls we get concern ground snakes. Far from dangerous, humans benefit from the presence of these natural pest control agents. They feed readily on cockroaches, crickets, scorpions, and spiders. Some individuals have uniform brown or orange backs, but others have a series of black bands, a trait which often causes them to be confused with coral snakes. ∿

LYRE SNAKE

Lyre snakes are one of several species of reptiles that utilize thin rock exfoliations on the surfaces of granite boulders. The sun's heat penetrates the rock flake from the outside, warming the snake underneath. Unscrupulous collectors take advantage of this habit, using hands and pry bars to break rocks apart, uncovering and gathering reptiles for illegal sale in the pet trade. Broken pieces of rock collect at the bases of rock outcrops, leaving habitat that is unsuitable for former inhabitants like the lyre snake, rosy boa, chuckwalla, and night lizard. Under natural conditions, it may be several hundred years before cap rocks again crown these boulders and exfoliations hang on their sides. Will there still be lyre snakes to make use of them? ∿

JEFF HOWLAND

MEXICAN GARTER SNAKE

The Mexican garter snake is highly aquatic, preferring relatively still water. Most of its habitat in Arizona has been lost to development or invaded by bullfrogs and introduced predatory fishes. They prey heavily on young Mexican garter snakes, leaving many remaining populations to consist largely of old individuals (some over three feet long), covered with scars from past encounters. Old snakes are dying more quickly than they are replaced by the few young snakes lucky enough to reach adult size. Many of the older snakes probably grew up on a diet of young leopard frogs and their tadpoles, and may not have noticed when their food base slowly shifted to bullfrogs. Adult leopard frogs, however, ignored the young snakes that the much larger adult bullfrogs devour. ∿

MOHAVE RATTLESNAKE

Foraging behavior of a Mohave rattlesnake consists of waiting, coiled under a bush beside a trail with fresh rodent scent. At night, when illumination is inadequate for its eyes, infrared sensing pits can detect the body heat of a kangaroo rat several feet away. With head turned toward the unsuspecting prey, bringing both pits to bear, accuracy of depth perception nearly matches that of its eyes in daylight. When the kangaroo rat moves within striking distance, several inches from the snake's nose, it strikes quickly, hitting the prey at mid-body. The kangaroo rat jumps, crawls several feet on wobbly legs, and dies. The snake crawls out of its coil, moving its head from side to side, tongue flicking, until it finds the chemical trail leading to its meal. ∿

JEFF HOWLAND

NARROW-HEADED GARTER SNAKE

For those who frequent freshwater habitats of the eastern United States, water snakes are a familiar site. We have none in Arizona, but the narrow-headed garter snake is, in many ways, more similar in appearance and ecology to water snakes than to other garter snakes. This highly aquatic snake is found in unimpounded, fast flowing rocky streams of the White Mountains and Mogollon Rim. It is just one of many species threatened by loss and disruption of Arizona's sensitive riparian habitats. It has suffered from declines in its natural prey base of native fishes and leopard frogs. Introduced predatory fishes and habitat loss from dams, stream diversion, logging, and other human activities have also taken their toll. ∿

JEFF HOWLAND

NIGHT SNAKE

JEFF HOWLAND

The night snake is one of the most widely distributed of Arizona's snakes. It occurs in virtually every habitat with the exclusion of spruce-fir forests. Night snakes spend daylight hours sheltered in crevices or beneath surface debris and are often common residents of desert trash piles. They feed on smaller reptiles and amphibians which are found during their nocturnal forays. Night snakes are among several species of rear-fanged snakes that are mildly venomous, but harmless to humans. They are a major predator of night lizards and banded geckos. Studies have shown that the tail-waving behavior of geckos is an effective defense against night snake predation. When disturbed, these small snakes often coil tightly and flatten their head, striking an imposing form. 〰

REGAL RINGNECK SNAKE

JOHN LOFGREEN

The regal ringneck snake is one of Arizona's prettiest snakes. It lives in grasslands, high desert riparian areas, chaparral or oak, and pine woodlands. Ringneck snakes prey on other reptiles (they have a particular fondness for other small snakes), amphibians, and occasionally newborn rodents. They are secretive and seldom encountered. When frightened by a predator, a ringneck snake displays the brightly colored underside of its tail, coiled in a cork-screw fashion. At the same time, the snake's head is often hidden beneath its coils. Perhaps this flash of color redirects the predator's attack to the tail and cloaca, giving it a mouthful of foul anal secretions (a common defense among snakes) and causing it to lose its appetite. 〰

ROSY BOA

The rosy boa is the only boa native to Arizona and one of only two in the U.S. At 3 feet long, this docile snake of our rocky desert mountains is not what most people think of when they hear the name "boa." Rosy boas are slow, often moving with body stretched in a straight line, the belly scales pushing it along. This is called rectilinear locomotion. The more common undulatory or serpentine locomotion employed by most snakes is much faster and boas switch to it for quicker movements. When harassed, the "Rosy" may roll up into a tight ball for protection. Males move considerable distances on spring evenings, following the pheromone trails of females. After a four to five month gestation period, females give live birth. ᳁

GEORGE ANDREJKO

SADDLED LEAF-NOSED SNAKE

Two species of leaf-nosed snakes occur in Arizona, but the natural history of neither one is very well known. Much like its cousin, the spotted leaf-nosed snake, the saddled species occurs in desertscrub (from creosote bush flats up into saguaro-paloverde covered foothills) on rocky or sandy soils. Leaf-nosed snakes are fossorial and are believed to feed mainly on lizards and their eggs. The saddled leaf-nose is most often seen crossing roads in late spring or after the summer rains begin, especially on paved highways west of Tucson and southwest of Phoenix. But even on a road, its desert colors and small size (anything over a foot is a monster) makes it easily over-looked, especially by those who are driving faster than about 25 mph. ᳁

RANDY BABB

RANDY BABB

SONORAN MOUNTAIN KINGSNAKE

Sonoran mountain kingsnakes are serpents of mountain woodlands and canyons, sometimes following riparian corridors down into desert grasslands. They can be fairly common in drainages descending from the Mogollon Rim and the higher mountain ranges of southeast Arizona. Large numbers sometime occur in small pockets of habitat, usually at rock outcrops. The same individuals can be found at nearly the same spot year after year. Mountain kingsnakes prey on birds, small mammals, and other reptiles, especially lizards. Because of their beautiful coloration, they are highly prized in the world of reptile keepers. Ironically, many aficionados use unethical collection methods that result in permanent damage to the rocks and downed wood favored as hiding places. Sometimes these practices severely impact local populations of the animals they love. ✓✓✓

HOWARD LAWLER

SONORAN WHIPSNAKE

A Sonoran whipsnake may often spend the morning crawling through a boulder field on a steep hillside. It sticks its nose into every crack, flicking its tongue, seeking the telltale chemical signals emitted by the lizards and small rodents it eats. It crawls into crevices, ignoring crickets and spiders clinging to vertical walls. It may even be chased from a cavity by an irascible mother woodrat. Finding a meal, like a large desert spiny lizard caught in its refuge from the late morning sun, may take several days of active search. The snake then retreats to a comfortable spot deep in a crevice, hidden from all but the faintest glimmer of the bright day. It stays there several days, digesting its meal, before venturing forth again. ✓✓✓

RANDY BABB

SOUTHWESTERN BLACKHEADED SNAKE

Arizona's four (possibly five) species of blackheaded snakes strongly resemble each other. Species are identified by the configuration of the black cap on the head and the detailed anatomical structure of the males' reproductive organs. Southwestern blackheaded snakes are by far the most common and widespread of Arizona's blackheaded snakes. They are small and secretive snakes that are seldom encountered, mainly because they spend most of their time burrowing through lose soil or tunnels constructed by other animals. Blackheaded snakes occasionally wander into homes, especially during spring and late summer. But don't worry, they are completely harmless to humans. They prey upon a variety of small invertebrates, including centipedes and spiders, that you may not want around your house anyway. ✓✓✓

STRIPED WHIPSNAKE

Moving across its favored desert slopes and canyon bottoms, a male striped whipsnake is always alert. Its large eyes are particularly sensitive to movement and its chemosensory organs search for the scent of prey or mates. When the trail of another snake is detected, he determines whether it was left by another striped whipsnake and, if so, he can discern its sex. If the trail was left by a sexually receptive female, he tracks her down. If another male is present, combat ensues. The larger male generally chases the smaller away and courts the female. If they mate, the male may remain near her for several hours or even a few days, guarding her from the advances of competing males, increasing the likelihood that any offspring will be his. ᗐᐧ

GEORGE ANDREJKO

TIGER RATTLESNAKE

In comparison to most other species of rattlesnakes in Arizona, the tiger is not often seen, at least not anywhere except the base of the Tucson Mountains. The tiger is most common in low, rocky Sonoran desertscrub of south-central Arizona, from Phoenix south to Mexico. Its grayish to pinkish body, conspicuously banded with tiger "striping," is closely matched to the soils on which it occurs. The tiger has a remarkably small head that is not even twice as wide as its rattle! Possessing a rather potent venom, though in small supply, the tiger preys on small mammals as an adult. The youngsters find lizards more to their liking. ᗐᐧ

RANDY BABB

WANDERING GARTER SNAKE

The wandering garter snake is the most commonly seen snake near water in the high country of central Arizona. One of the most interesting paternity assurance mechanisms ever evolved is found in garter snakes. At the end of copulation, the male deposits a mucilaginous plug in the cloaca (common opening of the digestive and urogenital tracts) of the female. This functions like a chastity belt, freeing the male to pursue additional mates while leaving the female unable to mate with subsequent suitors. The plug breaks down within a few days, after fertilization has occurred, and a few months later the female gives birth to a brood of little snakes, all fathered by a single male. ᗐᐧ

JEFF HOWLAND

WESTERN DIAMONDBACK RATTLESNAKE

GEORGE ANDREJKO

The danger and temperament of the western diamondback rattlesnake are the subject of a considerable body of folklore, most of it exaggerated. When not provoked or frightened, most individuals are not aggressive. Many do not even rattle when approached quietly. Rattlesnakes do not have especially acute vision and are probably deaf like other snakes. Being a pit viper, diamondbacks have facial pits lined with nerve endings that detect infrared radiation. This is emitted by any object, the frequency a direct function of its temperature. The pits sense the contrast between warm-bodied animals and their cooler surroundings. Now used to locate prey, the pits may have evolved as a predator detection device. Rattlesnakes are preyed upon by many endotherms, including coyotes, badgers, hawks, and now humans. ᗯᕁ

WESTERN PATCH-NOSED SNAKE

RANDY BABB

Like whipsnakes, the western patch-nosed snake is one of few desert ophidians active primarily during daylight hours. Many diurnal snakes (such as whipsnakes, garter snakes and patch-nosed snakes) are striped. The striped pattern makes it difficult for predators to estimate the speed of their intended prey, causing them to misjudge their strike. They often miss entirely, pouncing at a spot where the snake passed a fraction of a second earlier. Patch-nosed snakes feed mostly on lizards, but may occasionally take small mammals and reptile eggs, unearthed with the help of the large, flat rostral scale on the tip of the nose. Actively foraging patch-nosed snakes usually flee from an approaching human and are non-venomous. ᗯᕁ

WESTERN RATTLESNAKE

The Western rattlesnake is the most variable of this country's venomous snakes. Five subspecies, each recognizable by color pattern, occur in Arizona. The salmon colored Grand Canyon rattlesnake is endemic here; the Arizona black and Hopi are nearly so. The different color patterns are reasonably well matched with regional differences in habitat, each subspecies cryptically colored on its favored substrates. Ten of Arizona's 11 species of rattlesnakes are distributed primarily in the southwestern half of the state, mostly in low elevation deserts and desert mountain ranges. Only the western rattlesnake is predominantly found in Arizona's northeastern half, over much of which it is the only venomous snake. It is found in mountains, high elevation deserts, and prairie habitats where it occurs across most of the western states. It is fairly easy to distinguish all subspecies of the western rattlesnake from our other large rattlers. The western diamond-back and Mohave both have bold black and white bands around the tail, while the black-tail lives up to its name. The western rattlesnake may have a banded tail, but the colors are more subdued and do not differ markedly from the coloration of the rest of the body. 〜

KEVIN ELLIS

WESTERN SHOVELNOSED SNAKE

Shovelnosed snakes live in loose soils, like wash bottoms or sand dunes. They "swim" through the sand in search of invertebrate prey, such as spiders, sand roaches, crickets, scorpions, and centipedes. In spring, shovelnosed snakes may hunt on the surface in the early evening. They often travel a circular route a few hundred yards long, returning to shelter just a few feet from where they emerged. This snake has a mild venom that is innocuous to humans but quite effective on its prey. Its bright coloration, including red bands bordered by yellow, causes confusion with the coral snake. However, the red (and sometimes black) bands do not entirely encircle the snake's body as they do in the coral snake, and the nose is light colored rather than black. 〜

RANDY BABB

Gambel's quail

Field Notes of Arizona
GAME SPECIES

BOB MILES

White-tailed deer

Normal Breeding Period: January

Young Appear: August

Average Number of Young: 2

Distribution: 4,000-10,000 feet in the central and southeast mountains of Arizona

Habitat: Oak-grasslands, chaparral, and pine forests

Food preferences: Weeds, shrubs, mast, grass, mistletoe, and cacti fruits in season

Size of Individual range: 4 square miles

Live Weight: Male — 125 lbs.; Female — 80 lbs.

Predators or enemies: Mountain lion, bobcat, eagle, and coyote

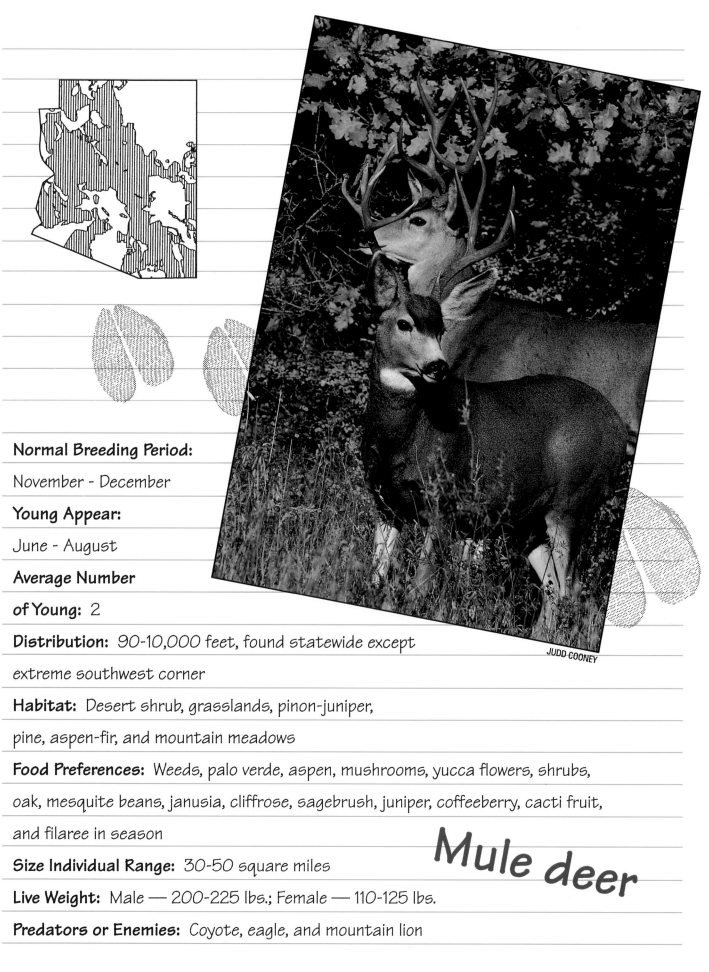

JUDD COONEY

Normal Breeding Period:

November - December

Young Appear:

June - August

Average Number

of Young: 2

Distribution: 90-10,000 feet, found statewide except

extreme southwest corner

Habitat: Desert shrub, grasslands, pinon-juniper,

pine, aspen-fir, and mountain meadows

Food Preferences: Weeds, palo verde, aspen, mushrooms, yucca flowers, shrubs,

oak, mesquite beans, janusia, cliffrose, sagebrush, juniper, coffeeberry, cacti fruit,

and filaree in season

Size Individual Range: 30-50 square miles

Live Weight: Male — 200-225 lbs.; Female — 110-125 lbs.

Predators or Enemies: Coyote, eagle, and mountain lion

Mule deer

Desert bighorn

GEORGE ANDREJKO

Normal Breeding Period:

September - November

Young Appear:

March - April or later

Average Number of Young: 1-2

Distribution: 90-4,500 feet desert ranges of southern and western Arizona

Habitat: Desert mountain ledges and grassy basins

Food Preferences: Fluff grass, catsclaw, ocotillo spurges, buckwheat, mescal, janusia, slim triodia, Indian wheat, filaree, and weeds in season

Size Individual Range: Extremely variable

Live Weight: Male — 250 lbs.; Female — 140 lbs.

Predators or Enemies: Eagle, coyote, and bobcat

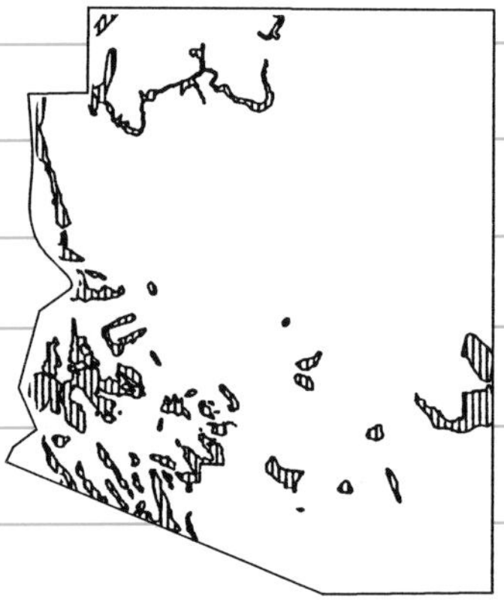

Elk

MICHAEL PELLEGATTI PHOTOS

Normal Breeding Period: September-October

Young Appear: June

Average Number of Young: 1

Distribution: 6,000-10,000 feet, northern Arizona

Habitat: Fir-aspen and pine-juniper forests

Food Preferences: Weeds, grasses, sedges, shrubs, willow, and trees in season

Size Individual Range: 20-30 square miles

Live Weight: Male — 900 lbs.; Female — 500 lbs.

Predators or Enemies: Mountain lion and coyote

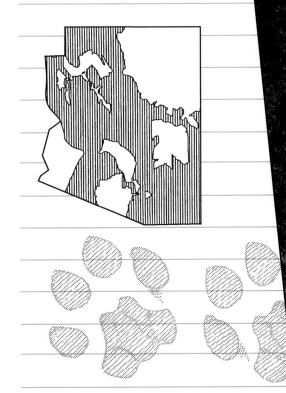

Normal Breeding Period: Year round

Young Appear: Year round

Average Number of Young: 2-4

Distribution: Found statewide except extreme southwest portions of the state

Habitat: Desert mountains with broken terrain and steep slopes

Food Preferences: Deer, elk, javelina, and livestock

Size Individual Range: Male — 20-150 miles; Female — 10-50 miles

Live Weight: Male — 80-150 lbs.; Female — 70-100 lbs.

Predators or Enemies: Practically none

MICHAEL PELLEGATTI

Mountain lion

Normal Breeding Period: Early July

Young Appear: January in hibernation

Average Number of Young: 2

Distribution: 4,000-10,000 feet,
forest areas throughout Arizona

Habitat: Chaparral pine forests
and aspen-fir pine forests

Food Preferences:

Omnivorous - berries, roots,
grass, cactus fruits, insects,
and occasionally livestock

Size Individual Range:

 7-50 square miles

Live Weight:

Male — 350 lbs.;

Female — 250 lbs.

Predators: Practically none

Black bear

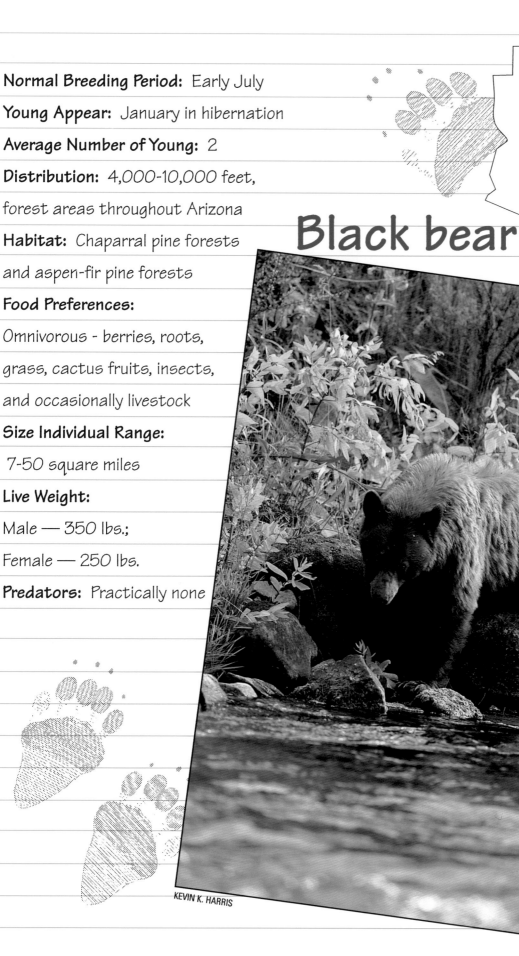

KEVIN K. HARRIS

Javelina

GARY KRAMER

Normal Breeding Period: Year round

Young Appear: Year round

Average Number of Young: 2

Distribution: 1,000-6,000 feet, mostly south of Mogollon Rim

Habitat: Desert, chaparral, and oak-grasslands

Food Preferences: Cacti, insects, fruits, and seeds in season

Size Individual Range: 4 square miles

Live Weight: Male — 65 lbs.; Female — 50 lbs.

Predators or Enemies: Coyote

MICHAEL PELLEGATTI

Antelope

Normal Breeding Period: August - September

Young Appear: May - June

Average Number of Young: 2

Distribution: 1,000-8,000 feet, grasslands of northern and southern Arizona

Habitat: Open grass and forest parks

Food Preferences: Grasses, weeds, cacti, juniper, winterfat, and chamiso

Size Individual Range: 20-40 square miles

Live Weight: Male — 110 lbs.; Female — 75 lbs.

Predators or Enemies: Eagle and coyote

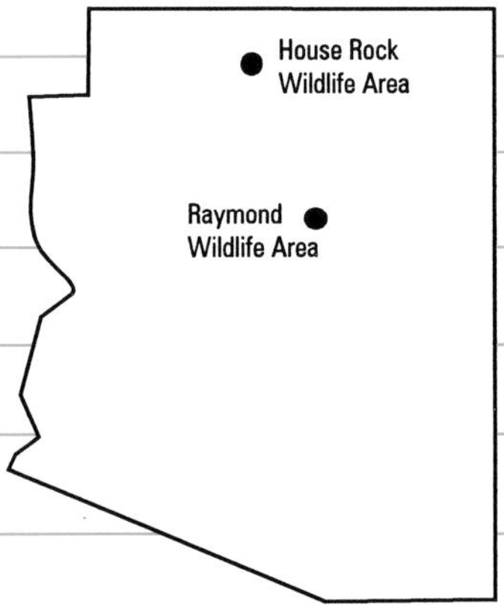

House Rock
Wildlife Area

Raymond
Wildlife Area

MICHAEL PELLEGATTI

Buffalo

Normal Breeding Period:

Mid-July to early September

Young Appear: Late April - May

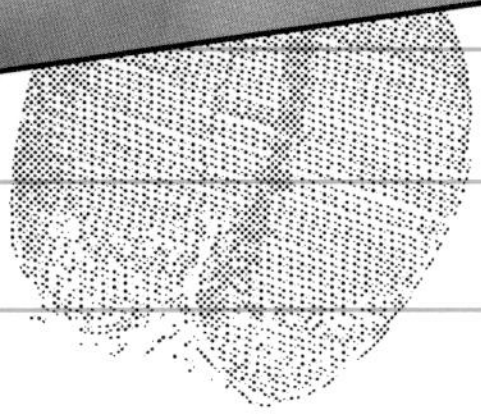

Average Number of Young: 1

Distribution: Found on Game and Fish properties — Raymond Ranch and House Rock wildlife areas

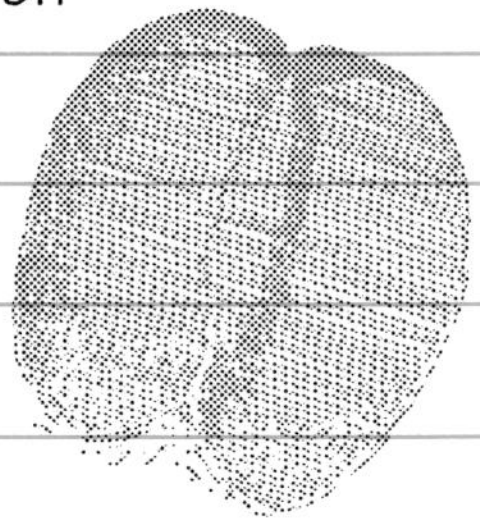

Habitat: Grasslands of northern Arizona

Food Preferences: Grasses and forbs

Live Weight: Male — 1,400-2,500 lbs.; Female — 750-1,600 lbs.

Predators or Enemies: Mountain lions attack calves; practically none for the adults

Turkey

MICHAEL PELLEGATTI PHOTOS

Normal Breeding Period: Late April - May

Young Appear: June

Average Number of Young: 9

Distribution: 5,000-9,000 feet along the Mogollon Plateau and White Mountains

Habitat: Pine forests

Food Preferences: Green weeds, insects, juniper berries, acorns, grass seed, mast, and pine seeds

Size Individual Range: 5-30 square miles

Live Weight: Male — 15-30 lbs.; Female — 8-12 lbs.

Predators or Enemies: Bobcats, coyotes, foxes, eagles, and great horned owls

GARY KRAMER

Sandhill crane

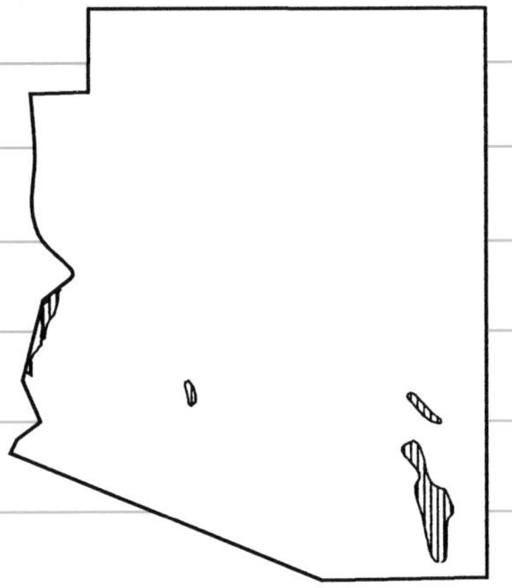

Normal Breeding Period: May-June (but does not breed in Arizona)

Young Appear: June - July

Average Number of Young: 1-2

Distribution: During the winter the majority roost on or near Willcox Playa in southeast Arizona, others found along the lower Colorado River, and lower Gila River

Habitat: Roost sites — alkaline depressions, marshy grasslands, and open shallow ponds; Loafing areas — wet, grassy meadows of sedges, spike-rush, and other short-statured marsh plants; Feeding - cultivated grainfields

Food Preferences: Corn, milo maize, newly planted winter wheat, oats, and lettuce

Size Individual Range: Migratory

Live Weight: 5 lbs. 4 ozs. - 14 lbs. 8 ozs.

Predators or Enemies: Coyotes and bobcats

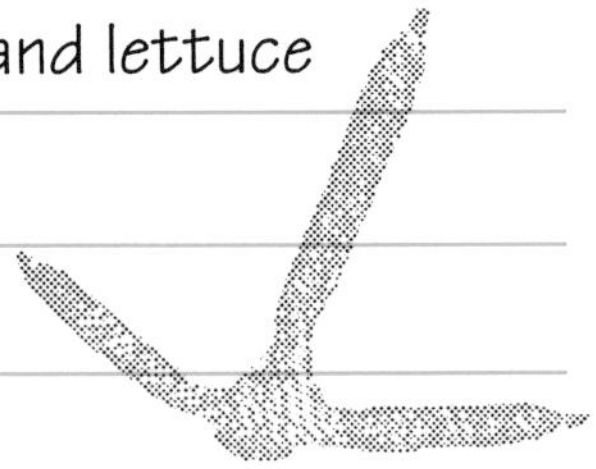

Ducks

Wood duck
MICHAEL PELLEGATTI

American wigeon
GEORGE ANDREJKO

Northern pintail
MICHAEL PELLEGATTI

There are approximately 20 species of ducks found in Arizona.

Normal Breeding Period: April - July

Young Appear: May - August   **Average Number of Young:** 6-10

Distribution: In Arizona's wetlands   **Habitat:** Wetlands

Food Preferences: Wood duck — seeds and mast found along waterways;

Northern pintail — grains; American wigeon — algae and duck weed

Size Individual Range: Varies by species

Live Weight: Wood duck — up to 1.5 lbs.; Northern pintail — 2-2.5 lbs.;

American wigeon — 1.5-2 lbs.

Predators or Enemies: Hawks, owls, eagles, foxes, coyotes, and bobcats

MICHAEL PELLEGATTI

There are four species of geese which migrate through Arizona.

Canada goose

Normal Breeding Period: April - July

Young Appear: May - August

Average Number Young: 6-10

Distribution: In Arizona's wetlands

Habitat: Wetlands

Food Preferences: Grains, grasses, and filaree

Live Weight: 2.5-15 lbs.

Predators or Enemies: Hawks, owls, eagles, foxes, coyotes, and bobcats

PAT O'BRIEN

Blue grouse

MICHAEL PELLEGATTI

Normal Breeding Period: May - June

Young Appear: June 15 - July 15

Average Number Young: 4-6

Distribution: 8,500 feet and above

Habitat: Subalpine fir and spruce forests and meadow regions of northern Arizona

Food Preferences: Insects, ants, grasshoppers, wild pea, raspberries, spiny gooseberries, dandelions, silverleaf, cinquefoil, aspen leaves, and Douglas-fir needles in season

Size Individual Range: Less than an acre to 2 acres

Live Weight: Male — 2-3 lbs.; Female — 1-2 lbs.

Predators or Enemies: Bobcats, coyotes, foxes, eagles, and great horned owls

Scaled quail

NORM SMITH

Normal Breeding Period: May - August

Young Appear: June - September

Average Number of Young: 7-14

Distribution: 3,000-6,000 feet in southeastern and eastern Arizona **Habitat:** Semidesert grasslands

Food Preferences: Tree and shrub buds, green weeds, insects, mesquite beans, mustards, miscel seeds, and cacti fruit in season **Size Individual Range:** 60-160 acres

Live Weight: 6-8 oz. **Predators or Enemies:** Hawks, foxes, ants, skunks, house cats, rodents, and snakes.

Montezuma quail
(Mearns' quail)

RICK BOWERS

Normal Breeding Period: Late February - March

Young Appear: July - September

Average Number of Young: 6-11

Distribution: 4,000-6,800 feet in southeastern portions of the state

Habitat: Madrean evergreen woodlands of oaks and pine

Food Preferences: Bulbs of wood sorrels, tubers of flat sedges, and insects

Size Individual Range: 60-160 acres

Live Weight: Male — 6.9 oz.; Female — 6.2 oz.

Predators or enemies: Hawks, foxes, ants, skunks, house cats, rodents, and snakes

Normal Breeding Period: April - June

Young Appear: May - July

Average Number of Young: 9-15

Distribution: 90-5,500 feet in

southern and western Arizona

Habitat: Grasslands and desert shrub

Food Preferences: Tree and shrub

buds, green weeds, insects, mesquite beans,

mustards, miscel seeds, and cacti fruit in season

Size Individual Range: 60-160 acres

Live Weight: 5-7 oz.

Predators or Enemies: Hawks, foxes, ants, skunks,

house cats, rodents, and snakes

Gambel's quail

JOHN CANCALOSI

Pheasant

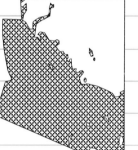

STEVE W. SMITH

Normal Breeding Period: April - May

Young Appear: Last weeks of May - June

Average Number Young: 8-14

Distribution: Scattered sites   **Habitat:** Humid river

valleys having small, irrigated farms with row crops of

alfalfa and grain bordered by unkept fence rows and citrus orchards

Food Preferences: Insects, cultivated greens and waste grain,

alfalfa and barley sprouts, kernels of maize, barley, and corn

Size Individual Range: Less than 5 acres

Live Weight: Male — 2 lbs. 8 oz. - 2 lbs. 10 oz.; Female — 1 lb. 14 oz.

Predators or Enemies: Bobcats, coyotes, foxes, eagles, and great horned owls

Mourning dove

JOHN CANCALOSI

Normal Breeding Period:

February 1 - September 15

Young Appear:

February - September

Average Number of Young: 1-2

Distribution: 90-9,000 feet

Habitat: Open thickets, farms, and desert

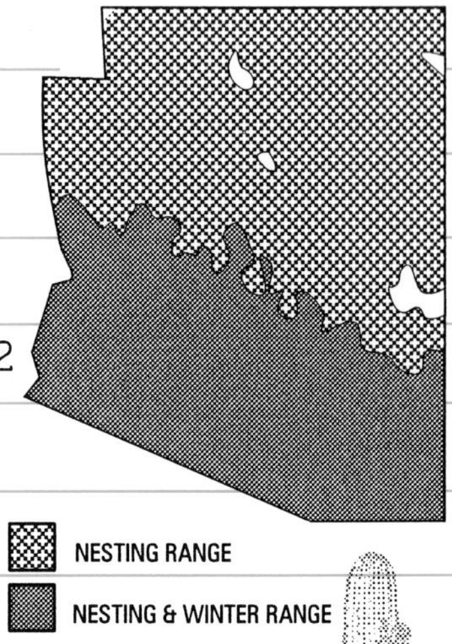

NESTING RANGE

NESTING & WINTER RANGE

Food Preferences: Weeds and grain seeds

Range: Migratory   **Live Weight:** 3-4 ozs.

Predators or Enemies: Hawks, owls, snakes, and scaly lizard

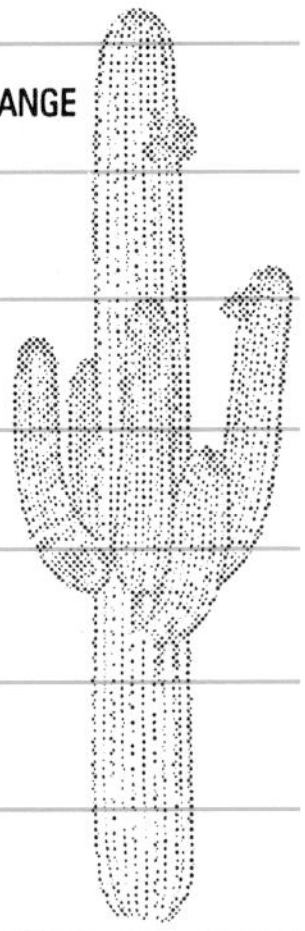

White-winged dove

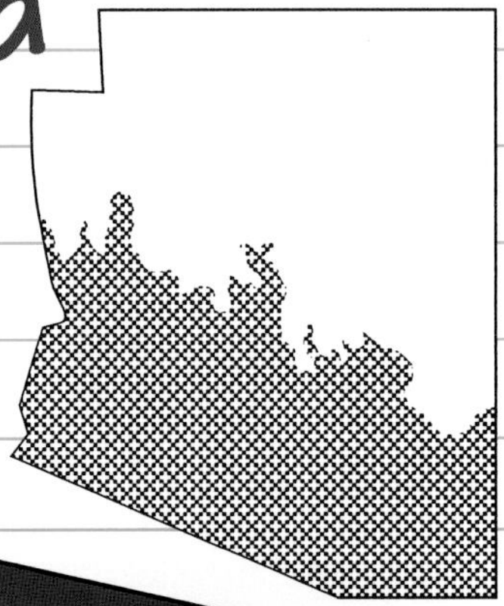

Normal Breeding Period:

May 20 - July 1

Young Appear: May - August

Average Number of Young: 2

Distribution: 90-5,000 feet in southern Arizona

Habitat: Mesquite bosques, desert, and all riparian systems

Food Preferences: Weeds, grain seeds and saguaro fruit in season

Size Individual Range: Migratory

Live Weight: 4-5 ozs.

Predators or Enemies: Hawks, owls, and snakes

GREG HOMEL

There are three species of cottontails and two species of jackrabbits in Arizona.

Desert cottontail

Normal Breeding Period: Year 'round

Young Appear: Year 'round

Average Number of Young: 3-7 **Litters Per Year:** 3-5

Distribution: 90-9,000 feet

Habitat: Desert, grasslands, farms, and pine-juniper forests

Food Preferences: Grasses, weed, cacti, bark, cultivated crops, and legume shrubs in season

Size Individual Range: 160 acres

Live Weight: Varies with species

Predators or Enemies: Snakes, foxes, coyotes, hawks, owls, and Gila monsters

Note: A hunting license is required to take any wildlife species in the state of Arizona. For more information, contact any Game and Fish Department office or consult the applicable regulation for the species you are interested in.